*A World
in Your Ear*

A World in Your Ear

The Broadcasting of an Era, 1923—64

ROBERT WOOD
M.V.O., F.R.S.A.

© Robert Wood 1979
Introduction © Robert Dougall 1979

All rights reserved. No part of this publication may be reproduced or transmitted, in any form or by any means, without permission.

ISBN 0 333 24310 2

First published 1979 by
MACMILLAN LONDON LIMITED
*4 Little Essex Street London WC2R 3LF
and Basingstoke
Associated companies in Delhi, Dublin,
Hong Kong, Johannesburg, Lagos, Melbourne,
New York, Singapore and Tokyo*

Typeset by
CAMBRIAN TYPESETTERS
and printed in Great Britain by
REDWOOD BURN LIMITED
Trowbridge and Esher

Contents

	List of Illustrations	7
	Foreword	9
1	Howls and Bangs in the Attic	13
2	May I Bring My Microphone?	34
3	Baldwin and the Boat Race	52
4	'Look after the king'	99
5	War of Words	125
6	Festival and coronation	152
	Postscript	173
	Appendix	178
	Index	189

This book is dedicated to
J.C.W.R.
and to my wife Barbara,
whose unfailing support
made everything possible

List of Illustrations

1. The author in 1921 with a receiver he designed and made.
2. Captain Peter Eckersley of the BBC.
3. J.C.W. Reith.
4. Installing an aerial at 2ZY in Manchester in 1924.
5. Dan Godfrey of 2ZY conducts an orchestra in the studio there.
6. The author at the controls of 2 ZY's transmitter.
7. Broadcasting Sir Alan Cobham's arrival from Australia by seaplane, 1926.
8. Neville Chamberlain returns from Munich in 1938.
9. Winston Churchill broadcasts in 1940.
10. The Crystal Palace fire.
11. King George VI's 1944 Christmas broadcast.
12. Princess Elizabeth and Princess Margaret.
13. The 1944 Christmas pantomime at Windsor Castle.
14. Richard Dimbleby in the commentator's box for the 1953 coronation.
15. The state procession after the ceremony.
16. Howard Marshall.
17. John Snagge.

Foreword

IT IS A PLEASURE to write these few words, although my first thought was that Robert Wood needed no introduction from me. I may have played a small part in encouraging him to go ahead with his book by pointing him in the direction of my literary agent, but his natural racy style inherited from a journalist father would, in any case, have ensured its success.

Engineers have always been the only wholly indispensible people in broadcasting, and yet to the general public their names are seldom well known. R.H. Wood is one of the all-time greats. From the moment he knocked on the door of the newly formed British Broadcasting Company in 1922 and met the boss — a certain Mr J.C.W. Reith — young Wood was in the forefront of all engineering developments. (Reith impressed him mightily: 'he made me feel like two threepenny bits.')

The new recruit was soon pioneering the broadcasts of all principal British occasions. So often was Robert Wood called to Buckingham Palace that it was no surprise when an equerry described him as one of the family.

In these pages we can now share with him the

A World in Your Ear

history he saw in the making. His intimate, modest and illuminating account deserves every success.

Robert Dougall

1

Howls and Bangs in the Attic

I was born in the 20th century, on 27 October 1903, but the world I grew up in was still, in essence, the world of the 19th. My father, Robert, was a journalist on a local newspaper, the *Buxton Advertiser*, at Buxton in the Derbyshire Peak District. And Buxton in those days was quiet and self-contained, a 19th-century spa that unfolded its wings in the summer months when the cotton magnates of Lancashire came to drink the mineral waters in the Pump Room and purge a winter's excesses, and closed them again during the winter months, when huge snowdrifts cut us off from the outside world.

The waters were supposed to cure rheumatism, but when I was taken to try them as a boy I thought the taste was so awful that if you were not ill when you came to Buxton, you would be after you had taken the cure. I did not care much for Buxton either. It was glorious in summertime. That I could acknowledge. But it was such a short summer. And I could never face another winter there now, with the thought of those snowdrifts. I was always ill with tonsillitis or something, though I've had scarcely a day's sickness since I left.

A World in Your Ear

But the world was about to break in and shake Buxton out of its calm. It began with the arrival of one man, an Italian known locally as Mr Froude. He came to live in the town and opened the great Ferodo brake-linings factory at Chapel-en-le-Frith nearby, providing a lot of local employment for people who until then had been farm labourers. We were still at the coach-and-horses stage, and he brought us abruptly into the world of the motor car.

I was on the edge of this, passionately interested in the arrival of the 20th century and all that I knew it would bring through the miracle of electricity. For I think I was born not with a silver spoon, but with an electro-magnet in my mouth. From the first I had itchy fingers for anything mechanical, but my obsession was with electricity. Other boys might want to be train drivers, and as a child I, too, made two mechanical steam engines for fun. But electricity was my passion.

I don't really know what started it. Not my father: he had no interest in such matters. Perhaps I got it from his father, for he was an engineer. He died when I was a child, but around the house we had some working models that my grandfather had made, and I admired them and have them still. From as early as I can remember I was always biased towards electricity. When I was quite small I was given a book called *How It Works*, which enthralled me, and in a short time I was counting the days each week till my copy of *Practical Mechanics and Electricity* arrived. All my early knowledge came from books and magazines.

Howls and Bangs in the Attic

Percival Marshall published some excellent handbooks on every aspect of electrical engineering — the electric motor, the battery, the generator — and I collected them.

I got my first chance to experiment when a friend of mine, Fred Burgess, and I went off one day to an auction at Hampson's Salerooms and nervously made a bid for two dilapidated telephones for a few pence we had been saving. It was unusual to find an old telephone in those days, for they were still very much an innovation. But we were lucky: someone had abandoned these and they gave us a marvellous storehouse of components.

We immediately set up a telephone link between Fred's house and mine, looping the cable through our neighbours' back gardens, and began to call each other up. I do not suppose we had anything very memorable to say, but the thrill of talking on our own home-made private line was enormous. The telephones also gave me a power supply at last. Our house in Grange Road, like most houses of the day, only had gas. There was no electricity supply, which was a serious handicap to my experiments. But included in the job lot we had bought at auction were four Le Clanché batteries. They had been standing neglected for some time, but I was able to overhaul them and they provided me, at last, with an electric power supply, though of limited capacity.

Fred and I went to the same boys' school though he was a little older than I. His father was the conductor of the orchestra that played in the Buxton

A World in Your Ear

Gardens for our rich summer visitors, and sometimes my parents would take me to the Sunday night concerts. But Fred and I used to slip outside when no-one was looking and have a bit of fun with the slot machines instead.

As a boy I was a bit of a loner. My sister Dorothy was four years older than I, and so as I was getting immersed in electricity she was becoming preoccupied with young men. I did not see much of my father; like most journalists he worked unsocial hours, tending to come home after I had gone to bed and be asleep when I got up. My mother, Elizabeth, was many years younger than my father, who had married very late, and I remember her chiefly as being a very practical person and very domesticated. But she and I used to have one great treat together. She would take me down to the Buxton Spring Gardens on a Saturday morning and sit with me there at the tables inside and buy me a slice of Victoria jam sponge and a small glass of port wine. I was about 12 or 14 at the time, and I used to love it. I am still fond of a glass of port, but I have never been a beer drinker. Another treat I recall was an uncle who used to come over regularly on Friday evenings and always slipped me a cigarette or two.

But I was always independent as a boy, forced to look to my own resources. That is how it was and I am glad of it. It made me able to manage on my own — and in a life that was to throw me alone into the presence of prime ministers and kings, that early grounding in self-sufficiency was a valuable

Howls and Bangs in the Attic

preparation.

The outbreak of World War I, when I was 11, caused ripples to reach even a backwater like Buxton. The first the townspeople really understood of it was when troops of wounded Belgian soldiers began to arrive to be nursed in the local hospitals. Being a spa, with plenty of hotels and boarding houses and a reputation as a health resort, Buxton soon became a receiving centre for the Belgian wounded. They came straight from the trenches, in a shocking state. They needed medical help at first, and later rest and the chance to recuperate. People who had, until then, felt rather cut off from the war hastened to offer their help, and I was caught up in it. My father was a keen photographer with his own dark room at home, and he often sold pictures as well as stories to the local and national press. He began to bring some of the Belgian soldiers home, just five or six at a time, on weekday evenings for a bit of entertainment. With his interest in photography, and my interest in anything mechanical, we soon hit on the idea of giving them a magic lantern show.

We had to use old-fashioned torch batteries for the projector since we had no electricity, and the screen was just a sheet pinned to the wall. The slides we showed were only the little ones you could buy in the shops for tuppence — animals, comic strips, or views: anything to amuse them, since most of the soldiers could not speak English and were finding their convalescence exhausting and sad, so far from their families. I used to put the slides in, flip them across with my finger slowly, waiting for the laugh, and then push them to the other side. It helped to pass the time for them, and they began to nickname me 'Cinema Bobby'.

But what really began to liven Buxton up was the arrival of the Canadian Army. They decided to open a base there, since the snow provided them with ideal training conditions; and the impact they made on the town with their new ideas, their free-and-easy ways and their money was rather like the effect the Americans had in the next war. They really shook up the population, men and women, and I thanked God for it, for to a boy of my age Buxton really seemed in need of a shake-up. Nothing was ever the same again there. The first direct benefit was that the Canadians built two toboggan runs and presented them to the town. At last someone had found a proper use for all that dreadful snow! I quickly added tobogganning to ice skating and roller skating as my favourite hobbies.

The war was to do more than enliven Buxton. It was about to play its part in changing the course of my life too. For in 1917 my father was approached by the *Sheffield Daily Telegraph*, who offered him a job in Sheffield and asked if he could join them as soon as possible. The war had taken so many young men that it had caused staff shortages, and this was a great opportunity for my father.

It was an even better opportunity for me. I thought it was too good to be true. I was only 14, but I knew exactly what I wanted. I had not made much progress at school. I was about average, it seemed, in ability, but all they taught was the three Rs; there was no proper science, still less any engineering. So when I heard we were moving to Sheffield I begged my father to let me leave school altogether and take instead an apprenticeship in electrical engineering with one of the big Sheffield steelworks.

He was unsure about the whole proposal. He had ambitions for me to follow him into newspapers, or at least to get a decent white-collar job where I could wear a suit and tie and cut a figure in the world. But I pestered and begged him, and in the end he consulted the headmaster of my old school, a very stern man with almost no imagination. He looked at me disapprovingly and said, 'He'll possibly do something with his hands — with a lot of further education.' It was pessimistic, and unfair really. But it convinced my father that I should be allowed my wish. And within a few months he had approached the chief engineer at Cammell Laird and persuaded them to accept me as an apprentice. It was like opening the gates of heaven.

Sheffield, when we arrived there in November 1917, was going hell for leather. Every steelworks and munitions factory was working flat out to keep up production for the men at the front, and the contrast with the rural calm of Buxton was stunning. Within a few days of arriving we experienced our first Zeppelin raid. The huge thing, looking just like a sausage, went by overhead, and I remember nobody bothered with it. They just said, 'Oh, that's a Zeppelin,' and that was it. I suppose they had got used to them, though not many got as far as Sheffield; but to us they seemed very frightening. What I remember most about the air-raids was the huge clouds of smoke that billowed from the furnaces, for when a raid was known to be imminent all the steelworks in Sheffield raced to feed their furnaces and soon a giant smokescreen belched out from the hundreds of factory chimneys — throwing up a filthy but effective barrier of soot.

But all this bustling activity meant one early blow for me. Every farmer and every farmer's son wanted to be a munitions worker and was crowding into Sheffield, so houses were at a premium. My parents thought themselves fortunate to find a rented house at 31 Everton Road in Hunters Bar. But I was heartbroken, for here again I found we had gas, and no electricity at all. So my early experiments were once more handicapped by the need to rely on batteries.

That was a small complaint, for within a few months I had said goodbye to my schooldays for ever and started work at Cammell Laird, and felt at last that I had my feet on the right path. It was a five-year training, covering electrical engineering, mechanical engineering, the drawing office, the test room, the foundry and the power station in turn. Four or five evenings every week I also went to Sheffield University to take a course leading to an Associateship in Electrical Engineering. (And in passing, I must pay tribute to the personal interest and direction I received from W. M. Gibbons, who was registrar there for many years.)

Howls and Bangs in the Attic

It was an abrupt change from school. I left home at 7.00 in the morning and made my way by tram across Sheffield to Grimesthorpe, over on the east side, where Cammell Laird, John Brown, Firth and all the other giant firms had their works. I would arrive back home again at 6.00, change into a clean suit and get to the university for lectures from 7.00 to 9.30 or 10.00. We worked on Saturday mornings too.

I realized at once that my parents were uneasy about my going out to work so early, like a common working man. There was such snobbery then, and it was felt to be an inferior occupation. But although they frowned on it, I persevered and went on with my apprenticeship. It was a long day and a long week. We apprentices were not encouraged to hang about or gossip among ourselves, and there were no tea-breaks. We were given a few shillings a week as a token payment and almost the only entertainment we could afford was a walk round the shops with a couple of friends on a Saturday afternoon and five Park Drive or Woodbine cigarettes on Friday night. On Sunday I did my homework for the university, and on Monday it all began again.

I learnt a lot about life, and what it was thought to be worth, as well as about electrical engineering, in my apprenticeship days. Life was cheap where the workers were concerned. I have seen a man run in his clogs to plug with a steel pole a furnace that had sprung a leak. Next thing, he would slip on the stone floor and, before anyone could help him, the molten steel would break through the hole and hit him and there would be a dreadful cloud of smoke and steam — and a vacancy.

And I have seen men working at an unprotected grindstone and seen it explode into hundreds of bits, and the nearest man's head maybe a hundred yards away. There was no compensation: perhaps a few shillings for the widow if the management was feeling generous. It was a hard road, on shillings for most people. We had to take our own lunches to work — there were no canteens then, of course — and when we clocked out in the evenings there was always a crowd of 30 to 40 ragged, barefoot children hanging round the gate whispering, 'Any bread, mister, do you have any bread left?', begging for our scraps. The men were paid their 17 or 18 shillings on a Friday night or Saturday and their wives would have to pledge their possessions at the pawnshop again on Tuesday, to be redeemed at the end of the week in an endless cycle of debt and deprivation.

I almost lost my own life in an accident at work when, at about 16, I was given a job that should never have been given to an apprentice. There was a problem because one of the traversing cranes in the foundry seemed to be going slow, and the chargehand said, 'Wood, go up and take a tachometer and watch and check the speed of that motor.' So I climbed up on to this great crane as it slowly crossed the works floor carrying its load of molten steel in the giant ladle, and began to check the revolutions of the driving motor against the second hand of my watch. I was totally absorbed, concentrating on my task, and

Howls and Bangs in the Attic

completely unaware of the movable steel girders that ran at intervals across the roof. As the crane moved slowly forward, one of these cross-girders was coming closer and was about to take my head from my shoulders. Suddenly I felt a sharp painful blow on my leg that knocked me down to my knees, off balance. At that second the girder passed overhead, missing my scalp by inches. I looked down and saw the shop steward, Jack Pointer, who had seen what was happening and, in lightning response to the situation, had thrown a hammer at me to attract my attention. Luckily his aim was sure: I still have the scar on my leg.

I went down at once and thanked him, and showed my appreciation by immediately joining the Electrical Trades Union as a student member. This was an act unheard-of from an apprentice and word of it went right through the works: I think Cammell Laird thought the revolution was coming. But the experience made me a bit bloody-minded.

On the whole the training was teaching me self-sufficiency. I was 14 when I began, though I think that perhaps in looks and ways I may have seemed older. And coping with the adult working world at that age gave me a lot of confidence in later life. Staff control, or tricky assignments — and some of the things I was asked to do in later years seemed almost impossible — did not worry me too much because I always felt I could cope. I had learnt to rely on myself and do things my own way and, in the breathtaking years ahead, the knowledge steadied me.

A World in Your Ear

I found it hard at first to make friends in Sheffield. It was such a busy place with the war on, and, although there were a few other apprentices, we were all working so hard, in separate parts of the works, that it was difficult to find time or opportunity to gossip and get to know each other. I was not leading the typical schoolboy life of my contemporaries, yet was not old enough to join the men as an equal. Reginald Ratcliffe became my great friend, and in our spare time we would go for walks together. But he was busy studying like me, and taking the same classes as me, so we were a bit competitive too. Sometimes I would grow restless: it would begin to seem all work with no time for pleasure or sport. Then I would climb the high walls of the works and watch the Flying Scot locomotives roaring past, bound for London or the north. I watched the businessmen on board, sitting at luxurious ease in the restaurant car eating their toast while the world flew past outside, and I vowed to myself that one day I would travel in the same style.

By the time I was 17 I had picked up a considerable knowledge of electrical engineering and decided to apply for my first radio receiving licence. In those days you could not just buy a radio and switch on. You had more or less to build it yourself from various components, and then ask the Post Office for permission to tune in. There were no programmes, no music, no voices even, back in 1919 and 1920. The ether was saturated with morse signals, and they came over a very wide range of frequencies, from transmitters at

Howls and Bangs in the Attic

home and abroad.

By 1921 I had constructed many simple one- and two-valve receivers, and I'm afraid I was often late for my university lectures in the evening because I'd been sitting in the attic at home listening to one or other of the experimental stations. Early in 1922 I knew that broadcasting in the real sense had started. A voice from my receiver proclaimed: 'This is Two Emma Toc calling, Eckersley W-R-I-T-T-L-E calling.' It was Captain Peter Eckersley making the first broadcast from the experimental broadcasting station built by the Marconi Company at Writtle near Chelmsford. Within a matter of months I also heard another voice: 'This is Dr A. P. M. Fleming and Kenneth Wright calling. This is 2ZY, the Metropolitan Vickers Trafford Park experimental broadcasting station.' So Manchester was on the air too. These voices coming over the ether were the most exciting thing I had ever known. I used to listen, tense with anticipation and excitement, and sick when I had to tear myself away to rush over to my classes. I waited impatiently for the vacations between June and September, when I could listen in without having to keep one eye on the clock.

I soon began to write to Captain Eckersley and Dr Fleming at the experimental stations, sending them reports on how well their signals had been received in my area. Eckersley, in particular, captured my imagination. He was a brilliant radio engineer, but also a tremendous personality, and from the beginning seemed determined that the radio experiments should

A World in Your Ear

entertain. His half-hour evening programme – all the Writtle station was allowed to transmit at first – included gramophone records and talks, plays (complete with primitive sound effects) and even concerts. By now I was listening on a four-valve set which I had built myself, and my sister Dorothy called me a lunatic for 'messing about in the attic with howls and bangs and whistles'. But I was absorbed.

One problem faced by all early listeners was how to tune into different wavelengths to pick up the different signals. There was no dial to turn on those early sets; you had to juggle with some sort of commercial tuner, a coil, a needle, a bobbin or a condenser, but they were fragile and cumbersome. I thought about this a lot, and eventually invented my own solution. I began by constructing an ebonite tube about the size of a fat reel of cotton. Around this I wound double cotton-covered fine-gauge copper wire, counting the number of turns on the spool with the help of an ordinary revolution counter. The more turns, the longer the wire and the longer the wavelength to be received. I made various coils, of perhaps 25–75, 75–150, 150–300 and 300–500 turns, then coated them with shellac varnish and mounted them on a special two-pin electrical plug. Now, when I wanted to change wavebands, all I had to do was unplug one coil and plug in another; it was swift and reliable, and I used these plug-in coils for years. So did many other people: photographs of me and my invention, taken by my father, appeared in various technical magazines, and soon a number of shrewd

Howls and Bangs in the Attic

commercial copies were on sale, but alas with no financial benefit to me.

My hobby met with neither sympathy nor enthusiasm at the workbench. I used to experiment in my spare time there, during lunch breaks or after work, making my components and struggling to think of new refinements, but got into hot water when I stood there making little crystal detectors. One of the huge Scots foremen (Cammell Laird, not surprisingly, had a great many Scots foremen, and formidable people they were too) came up to me regularly and would say, 'Don't mess about with that damned nonsense. Nothing will ever come of it'.

But change was in the air, in the most literal sense. I used to read all the electrical papers to see what was going on, and it had been fairly generally leaked late in 1922 that six of the major electrical and radio manufacturing organizations were combining to form the British Broadcasting Company. It was the world I longed above all to join, so I sat down one Sunday afternoon, the only time in the week I had free, and wrote a letter to the chief engineer of the new company, offering my services in any capacity. The reply came from Captain Peter Eckersley, whose voice I knew so well from the Marconi broadcasts. He was now chief engineer of the new broadcasting company, and he wrote inviting me to an interview in London.

I had to take the day off from Cammell Laird without telling them what it was for, as I knew they would say I was being foolish because broadcasting was all rubbish. My father also wondered what on earth I was doing, but he subbed me for the fare, and my parents both saw me off on the early morning train to London in the one suit I had for university, a white collar and my best tie.

I'd never been to London before, and it must have shown in my face as I walked out of the station, because when I took a taxi from King's Cross to the BBC's offices, which were then on the top floor of 2 Savoy Hill, in the Institute of Electrical Engineers building on the Embankment, the driver took me on a tour of London, dropping me with only minutes to spare before my interview.

I walked inside and asked the commissionaire for the British Broadcasting Company. He sniffed and directed me disdainfully to a lift, saying there was some sort of radio company upstairs. I found the door, knocked and went in and found myself face to face with the genius called Captain Eckersley. He was a charming, humorous man, quite young himself, who put you at your ease immediately. He asked me what I'd done, and what I knew about broadcasting. I told him how I listened to broadcasts from Writtle and Manchester, and corresponded with the stations. And I added, 'When it really starts we shall know something,' for I was quite certain that broadcasting was of immense importance.

He seemed pleased with my enthusiasm and we chatted for a bit. Then he said, 'Now you'll want to meet the boss.' He got up and went over to an alcove that was curtained off from the rest of the room, and

Howls and Bangs in the Attic

pulled the curtain aside.

'This is Mr J.C.W. Reith,' he said, and from behind the desk where he was working stood the tallest man I had ever seen. He was enormous, six foot six, and made me feel like a couple of threepenny bits. And he had the most penetrating gaze of anyone I had ever met: his eyes looked right through you, seeing straight to the core with no nonsense. Reith talked to me for a while, and that was that. The whole interview lasted only about 15 or 20 minutes. I got a taxi that took me back to King's Cross in only a matter of minutes, making me realize how I had been duped on my first journey, and caught the same train back to Sheffield that I had arrived on earlier that morning.

My parents denounced the whole expedition as a waste of time and money, and, though I had been as thrilled as a schoolboy to meet the famous Captain Eckersley, and amazed and rather overawed by his huge boss, I felt a little disappointed myself.

However, I was now promoted at Cammell Laird, to the power station. I had also attracted a bit of attention during my apprenticeship for my particular ability in electrical matters. Four of the electrical engineers there, Messrs Gilberthorpe, Machin, Knight and Bell, were especially helpful. When Mr Nelson, a highly qualified engineer later knighted for his achievements in the electrical and mechanical world, visited the works, he sought me out because he had heard of my special interest in electrical affairs; he gave me a personal pep-talk and kindly nominated me to become a student at the Institute of Electrical

Engineers. His recognition of my studies, and his encouragement, meant a great deal to me. Recently I met his son, the present Lord Nelson, who is chairman of GEC, and I was able to tell him what a boost his father's interest had given me at that moment in my career.

Now my job was as a power station assistant, keeping an eye on the meters and dials that controlled the tapping of the furnaces and the travelling cranes that carried the great ladles of molten steel from the furnaces to the presses. I was kept on my toes monitoring a situation that changed constantly and was always potentially dangerous, and thought that my future was now decided: I was to be a power-station engineer.

I turned my thoughts to my private life. Two years earlier, in June 1921, at the age of 17, I had fallen head over heels in love. The girl's name was Barbara and, when we met, she was staying with her uncle and aunt in the Isle of Man on holiday. I was there with my parents, for I had been feeling the need of a break from the endless round of work and study, and as I had never been to the Isle of Man my parents decided to take me there.

It was a marvellous summer that year, and I felt wonderful, being free just to enjoy myself for a few days. I had been there a week when another couple arrived at the hotel, bringing with them their 16-year-old niece. This aunt and uncle were a charming pair and they soon became friends with my parents and started to go about with them. And I was dazzled by Barbara. We had only one week of our holiday left, and I thought I couldn't afford to waste time; so one day I plucked up my courage and said: 'Well, shall we have a walk about then?' She agreed, and for the first time we had a few minutes to ourselves. I asked her where she came from and my heart fell when she replied, 'Bangor, Northern Ireland.' I told her that I came from Yorkshire, and it seemed so far from Sheffield to County Down.

But I had been hard hit. When I got back home I began to write to her, although I was so busy. Eventually she wrote back, though not on the same scale: I wrote eight pages, she did one. But I persisted, and always swear that the lump I have to this day on my second finger comes from all that scribbling. I was still a student, of course, while her family, big, friendly and successful, owned a thriving fruit and fish business on the main street of Bangor. My future outlook can hardly have seemed very cheerful to them, but they did nothing to discourage her.

I was never one to give up if I could help it, and I won the next round, for I persuaded my mother and father to go back to the Isle of Man again the next year, and Barbara managed to persuade her brother and two friends to go there too. We could not co-ordinate our arrangements exactly, so although I was there for two weeks this time, we only overlapped by a week, but that was enough. Perhaps we risked disappointment by trying to repeat the past summer's feelings, but it did not turn out like that. I found I was as keen as ever, though nothing had changed. She still lived in Bangor and I was still at Cammell Laird, with my prospects no better than before.

In the summer of 1923, after my abortive trip to London, I faced a greater difficulty. My parents, not unreasonably, had refused to go to the Isle of Man yet again, and I was desperate about what to do. Then suddenly Barbara wrote to say that her parents had said I could go and stay with them in Bangor. I had not met them then, and no doubt they wanted to have a look at the youngster who was pursuing their young daughter with every sign of determination. So off I went to County Down to stay with them for a fortnight. I met a wonderful family, and found that Bangor was a beautiful seaside resort and yachting centre. Barbara's father was a keen sailor, and I began to enjoy a marvellous holiday. But somehow fate was determined that I should never have more than a few days together with Barbara, for I had been there less than a week when I received a telegram from my father telling me to return at once.

I caught the first boat back to Heysham and a train to Sheffield. My father met me at the station and handed me a letter. It was from Captain Peter Eckersley, appointing me as engineer to the new BBC station being set up at Manchester. I was to report on Monday 23 July, at a starting salary of £200: a large sum of money for a young man of 19 in those days, and approaching what my father was earning as a senior reporter.

I stood on the platform, clutching the letter,

Howls and Bangs in the Attic

paralysed. I thought, 'This is it, this is the start of everything I've ever wanted.' I could see that my father was very pleased. He thought it was really something worthwhile. He had not been able to telephone me with the news as the lines were so uncertain, but it was the one thing that could make leaving Barbara so soon seem worthwhile. I could hardly speak a word to anyone for hours. If the record *The Impossible Dream* had been available, and a gramophone, I would have played and replayed it a dozen times.

A day or so later I returned to Cammell Laird, told them I would be leaving, and collected my personal tools. They wished me well, though most of them thought I was launching myself into a very risky and uncertain future. A few days later I caught the early morning train to Manchester.

2

May I Bring My Microphone?

I came out of the London Road railway station in Manchester that July morning and set off to seek my fortune at 57 Dickenson Street. I had been to Manchester once or twice before. My mother and father often used to go there on a Saturday to shop, and it was in the Manchester department store of Lewis's that I had bought my first three-element valve, after successfully twisting my father's arm for the necessary few shillings.

Dickenson Street was easy to find because it was the site of a giant power station, whose tall chimneys were later enlisted to provide a handy support for my transmitter aerial. That morning I walked along and discovered that number 57 was the home of Calico Printers, a large industrial concern. The BBC had taken the top floor of what was really a rather sombre warehouse. Broadcasting had begun in Manchester in November 1922 in a small, famous, canvas-lined room in the research department of the Metropolitan-Vickers studios at Trafford Park, but in July 1923 it was decided to move to new studios in the heart of the city.

I walked into the gloom of the warehouse and

May I Bring My Microphone?

asked around for the BBC. A porter directed me to a contraption in the corner; it was a lift, or rather a hydraulic hoist, built to take a terrific weight and used to haul the bales of calico to the upper floors. I stepped in rather nervously and stood well back, since the thing had no doors at the front, and the porter tugged on a cable to start it off.

We came to a halt on the top floor, which was quite bare but crowded with unopened packing cases. I found one large room and other small rooms subdivided off, and a nucleus of staff. As I came out of the lift a man spotted me and introduced himself as the superintendent engineer, Mr J.C. Cameron, the BBC's representative. With him was Major Binyon, chief engineer of the Radio Communication Company, the firm supplying the transmitter, and one of his senior engineers.

I had no handbook and nobody had given me any information about the job. It was just a question of taking off our jackets and starting to open the packing cases under the keen eyes of the two RCC engineers. They were charming men who taught Mr Cameron and me a lot in a short time; it was fortunate because our transmitter was almost unique. All the other new BBC stations being set up at that time were using Marconi 'Q' transmitters. Ours was the only one using an RCC model, which was actually a converted ship's radio communication transmitter. For many years we were the only station equipped in this way and, being a one-off model, it was a little tricky and occasionally very temperamental.

A World in Your Ear

We began that day by deciding which room should be the studio and which the transmitting and control room. Then we knocked out a little window between them so that the engineer in the control room could see what was going on. Next we hunted for drapery to hang all round the bare warehouse walls to help make it soundproof and to improve the acoustics.

No-one had any idea at first what our hours of broadcasting would be. At that time they were limited by the Post Office to two or three sessions in the evening, say from 6.30 to 7.30, 8.00 to 9.00 and 9.30 to 10.00, with perhaps an occasional afternoon programme too. We discussed the likely hours on that first day, and I decided it would be easier to carry on living at home. I used to catch the 9.00 train to Manchester from Sheffield in the morning and the 10.00 train home at night, so my days were more or less from 10.00 to 10.00 in Manchester, and they went quite well.

We were all frantically busy at the beginning. If only the days had been twice as long I would have been a happy man. We each did as many jobs as we could, for we were working on a shoe-string. In those early days of 2ZY, the Manchester call sign, under Dan Godfrey and Victor Smithe, I often used to be roped in as Uncle Bob to read a story on what they called 'Children's Hour'. And once a month or so I used to give a little talk in the evening on the simple technicalities of radio — telling listeners how to construct a radio receiver or a crystal set — and was billed as 'The Professor', which I rather enjoyed.

May I Bring My Microphone?

I even found myself, on some hair-raising occasions, reading the news. We had one announcer there in the early days who sometimes had great problems with drink. He would go out during the evening break, take on more than he should and fail to turn up on time. We were so short-staffed that there were no stand-ins. So I would have to dash round into the studio and read the news myself, trying to keep an eye on the transmitter at the same time through the control-room window. On one memorable occasion he arrived back in the middle of this exercise, and I heard a lot of thumping noises and curses from down below. But I was able to put my hand into the hoist and clamp hold of the cable, leaving him stranded at the bottom kicking things around till the broadcast was over.

The lift itself was something of a problem. When we had performers coming into the studio in the evening, we used to pay the man who operated it during the day to work overtime and keep it going for our visitors. Many a time my colleagues and I would rush to drape it with curtains or odd bits of material — anything to cover up the bare-boned cradle and make it more presentable. We didn't want anyone sneering at our precious studio. We were young, exhausted and very content.

We were lucky that the studio was so close to Manchester's Oxford Street, where there was a splendid restaurant called the Palatine. It was a particular favourite, partly because it had a marvellous range of wines, but, even more important, because

A World in Your Ear

you could go there at almost any time and get a meal. In real emergencies they would send someone round with warm food for us. We were grateful, as it was often impossible to leave the studio for long.

It was a marvellous period. Experimentally, the sky was the limit. The Dickenson Street site had been chosen because it was central, and we used the prominent chimney stacks of the power station to attach a sloping aerial. When I started experimental transmission before the station opened, I was surprised to find from the postcards sent in by radio enthusiasts that we were even getting reports from America on our late-evening broadcasts. But electrical interference from the power station itself was a continual problem, and one that could only be solved by trial and error. Once broadcasting began, I used to give regular talks and ask people to report on the strength of the signal in their own area that night. In the morning, as the reports came in, I would mark the results on a huge architect's map of the Manchester region which I'd bought and hung on the wall in my office. Day after day I studied how best to improve the signal to districts where it was plainly weak. We were all thrilled with the idea of getting our broadcasts to the people and often worked through the night on a new idea.

In January 1924 I was able to make a dramatic improvement in the reception. Early morning shoppers in Oxford Street got a crick in the neck watching the sky. The object of interest was a huge new aerial which was being slung from the power station roof

May I Bring My Microphone?

by a team of dizzy engineers — headed by myself, trying very hard not to look down. Professional steeplejacks dismantled the old aerial and followed my instructions to fit a new design, shaped like a 'T' with an upright 200 feet high and a cross bar of 85 feet. Work began on dismantling the old aerial as soon as broadcasting had finished late one evening and the new one was ready and in operation in time for the first broadcast the following day.

At the beginning all broadcasting was done from our own studio. Our first station director was Dan Godfrey, son of Sir Dan Godfrey who was the leader and conductor of the Bournemouth Symphony Orchestra, and a distinguished musician in his own right. He was young too, only four years older than me, and he got on well with everybody. He used to conduct the most amazing orchestral pieces in our tiny studio. I remember one performance of *Madam Butterfly* he brought off, with the players and singers practically sitting on each other's knees. Dan was a strapping man who played rugby every Saturday, and he used to conduct these concerts dressed in his striped rugby shirt, standing in the scrum of musicians, gesticulating and encouraging, in a studio that grew steadily hotter and hotter.

He attracted some of the best musicians from the famous Hallé Orchestra to play in this crowded studio. Men such as Eric Fogg, Lionel Hirsch and their leader T.H. Morrison all took the hoist to our top floor. Their efforts were genuinely appreciated by an audience who had never before had the chance to

A World in Your Ear

hear music of such quality. Their feelings were caught in the local paper after a concert on 17 January 1924: 'Many phone messages were received last night and today by Mr Dan Godfrey expressing appreciation of his selection of two such noble works as "A Tale of Old Japan" [Coleridge-Taylor] and "Beethoven's Ninth Symphony"... congratulating him on the way in which their beauties were unfolded by the orchestra, principals and choir'. The paper's critic had been listening, like many others, on a crystal set, and was kind enough to praise, too, 'the quality of the transmission under the direction of Mr Wood'.

But I was already thinking of how to avoid the congestion in the studio by taking the microphone out to the orchestra. I began by discussing the idea with a group of senior Post Office officials in Manchester. My aim was to rent one of the best direct-routed wide-frequency telephone lines available, for an hour or two free from all interruption. Then I could take a microphone outside the studio to pick up the signal and send it down the line to the Dickensen Street transmitter for broadcasting to our listeners.

The GPO officials were most cooperative, and my next task was to try and establish contacts with all sorts of important people to win their permission to take my microphones to cover events that had never been broadcast before. But oh, the misunderstandings that arose. In the very early days few people had heard of broadcasting, and I would ring up a local town clerk or some other dignitary and say, 'I'm Mr Wood of the BBC and I'd like to talk to you if I

May I Bring My Microphone?

may' — only to be met with absolute bewilderment at the other end from someone asking, 'But what on earth does Battersea Borough Council want with us?' So every conversation began with an explanation of what the British Broadcasting Company was and what we hoped to do. Despite my youth and my inexperience at dealing with the high and mighty, I grew daily more fluent and persuasive.

Day after day we came up against the fact that we were pioneering — because, wherever we went, unless we were dealing with somebody very alive to the future, we were only tolerated. We were regarded as eavesdroppers: people were very suspicious of the microphone even 50 years ago, and wanted to know what it would pick up, what assurances I could give them that it would not be live when they were just having a gossip. And when I tried to take my microphone out to cover entertainment I met with even more hostility. The first reaction was often that the BBC would put everyone out of a job, close all the newspapers and put orchestras on the streets. In fact it *made* everybody, bringing fame to bandleaders and musicians who started to sell records and sheet music on an unprecedented scale, and kindling an interest in topical news that actually boosted newspaper sales; but naturally no-one was to know that at the beginning.

When I had won permission from everyone to attempt my first outside broadcast, I still faced the problem of finding the equipment to make it with. Money was very tight and everything was being done on a shoe-string. Our studio equipment was very simple: we had three American Western double-sided microphones, so that two people could sit either side of a single microphone and both be picked up. If I wanted one or two of these for an outside broadcast it became a case of snatch-and-grab: the studio would have to make do with only one or two, while I ran off with mine and returned it as fast as possible.

Luckily I found a small electrical and radio shop in nearby Oxford Street, run by an enthusiast called Mr Franks who was something of a radio pioneer. We had a small petty-cash float, and he would allow us to buy the components we needed on credit, making payments whenever the petty-cash float happened to have a bit to spare. Through his kindness and interest I was able to buy a single-stage loudspeaker amplifier which, with a little bit of modification, performed satisfactorily.

Our first outside broadcast was from the Oxford Street cinema, which had an orchestra playing daily at intervals between the silent films. I could only borrow one microphone from the studio, which made it quite difficult to get the right balance from the orchestra. But after trying it in various positions I achieved a reasonable sound. We set it up early in the morning and switched it on, then I went back to the studio. We sat in the control room at the selected time and waited. We had asked the conductor to tap with his baton on the case that housed the amplifier when he was ready to start. When we heard this tapping we made a swift announcement: 'Now we are

May I Bring My Microphone?

going over to the Oxford Street Cinema for some music,' and switched it over to him. When the concert had finished we faded it out, and later the same day I removed the microphone and amplifier and returned them to the studio. It was a success, and concerts from that cinema and others soon became a regular feature of our broadcasts.

Little by little, using loans and credit, I managed to pick up little transformers and odd little valves and batteries to build up three or four sets of outside broadcast equipment. The money came from licence fees — in those days ten shillings — and from money contributed by the half dozen or so major companies (such as GEC, Marconi and Ferranti) that had sponsored the setting up of the BBC.

After our success with the Oxford Street cinema, nothing could stop me. I was soon arranging direct broadcasts from the organ of the Piccadilly cinema and the orchestra of the Midland Hotel, and broadcasting the marvellous Hallé Orchestra straight from the Free Trade Hall. I was still forced to catch the balance of each orchestra as best I could with a single microphone, but there was no doubt of the audience's enthusiasm for what we were offering.

Yet even in those early days, one problem had emerged. Every door you open allows a few rogues to slip through; and from the beginning we had to watch out very carefully for unscrupulous song-plugging. In the early days the only records on sale were of the 'Land of Hope and Glory' and 'Sunday Night at the Pub' variety. It was radio that made popular music popular, which was why a band in those days turned up at the studio in evening dress. We were making the reputations not only of the musicians but of the composers too — and promoters would think nothing of slipping the conductor a few pounds to play some slow-selling song. So from the first we tried to see that the unscrupulous ones did not get an unfair share of air time.

Another of our pioneer ventures in those early days was to help launch two local relay stations. Local radio may be thought to be a modern craze, but within months of starting up 2ZY in Manchester we set up two more stations. One was in Liverpool, over a cafe in Lord Street, and the other was above the Union Grinding Works in Sheffield. They were small booster stations, each with a junior station director reporting to Dan Godfrey. They took the bulk of their programmes from 2ZY, but they also each had a small studio from which they could transmit local news and local items. To be one of the people involved in this pioneering work, bringing broadcasting out of the nursery and into the mainstream of affairs, was all that I had ever dared dream of being involved in, and I could scarcely believe my luck.

I was restless to extend my outside broadcasts to the limit. In May 1924 I decided it was time to move outside the Manchester area, and I planned our first successful broadcast from the Lancashire seaside resort of Southport. By this time we had our own 2ZY Orchestra, made up of local musicians, and we

May I Bring My Microphone?

had been approached by a musician called Klinton Sheper, a singer who had broadcast regularly from Manchester, asking if we would give a concert at the Cambridge Hall in Southport to raise funds for the Southport Infirmary.

Dan Godfrey was enthusiastic about the idea. It was already a rule that our orchestra would only give concerts outside the studio if they were in aid of charity, and this sounded very suitable. I was sent up to Southport to arrange the transmission using a rented GPO line to the Manchester transmitter. On 10 May the broadcast went off — without a hitch. And a newspaper commentator noted one detail that had astonished many people, the fact that the music was 'received by local "listeners-in" even before it had been heard at the back of the hall. These are indeed wonderful days'.

The concert was conducted by Dan Godfrey in what the same commentator called his 'stately yet picturesque' style, just a few days before he left us to become musical director of the 2LO station in London. And just one week later I was off again, this time to Morecambe, to broadcast the choirs from the Morecambe Musical Festival. This time I had managed to borrow two microphones, a great luxury. One was suspended by wires from the balconies just a few feet from the platform and only a little higher than the heads of the competitors. The other was attached to a music stand on the platform, for announcements. Sitting close by, I could switch from one to the other. The signal was then sent by GPO landline 50 miles to

45

Manchester for transmission. The broadcast was also relayed by landline to the BBC station at Aberdeen, where it was transmitted not only to a good part of Scotland, but to Scandinavia and North America too if atmospheric conditions allowed. The festival was estimated to have been heard by a million enthusiasts in Europe and America, a huge step forward from those crowded studio concerts of only a few months earlier.

Music was the natural first choice for us when we moved out of the studio. But I was equally keen to record all the events of the day. Pressure from the newspaper proprietors at that time meant we were not allowed to cover news events, but other interesting occasions were open to us: I seized the chance to introduce a new note, and encourage our supporters, by organizing live broadcasts from the first-ever British wireless exhibition, held at Manchester City Hall from 14 to 25 October 1924, sponsored by the *Manchester Evening Chronicle*. I also gave a little lecture at the exhibition on what went on behind the scenes at 2ZY, illustrated — shades of the Belgian wounded — by lantern slides thrown on to a screen as I talked. I was becoming quite an experienced lecturer by now. I gave a series of lectures on the BBC at Liverpool University under the chairmanship of Dr Eccles, at Manchester College of Technology under Dr Palmer, and at the renowned Atheneum Club, Manchester, where I was elected an honorary member and gave regular lunch-time talks.

Our success with outside broadcasts made us

May I Bring My Microphone?

determined to branch out further. There were so many possible venues within easy reach of Manchester: I began to look around. There was a wonderful flower show every year in Lord Street, Southport, with a band playing. We soon had a microphone fixed up. There was that marvellous place Blackpool, just up the coast, with its tower, its summer variety theatres, its crowds. Up to Blackpool we went.

Then came a bigger test. We were given permission to do a live broadcast covering the unveiling by Lord Derby of the Manchester War Memorial in St Peter's Square. The fact that we were allowed to take our microphones to cover so important and serious an event was a tribute to the success our outside broadcasts had achieved so far, a recognition that we could give our listeners a true understanding of the occasion. The whole ceremony was broadcast live, years before the Cenotaph ceremonies in London got underway, and I began to be gripped by the possibilities of outside broadcasts — the balancing-act that was required, the technical challenges, the ingenuity, the excitement and the independence of the job.

But an even more momentous event was on the horizon. I was still writing furiously to Barbara, and she was still writing back briefly but encouragingly. One day I just took a weekend off, headed off to Liverpool, caught the Irish boat and went to see her. I proposed almost as soon as I landed and was accepted.

Now I was engaged I had to think more carefully about the future. I had become aware through the BBC grapevine that there were plans to build an

A World in Your Ear

enormous high-powered transmitter for long-wave transmission, somewhere in the Midlands. This meant hundreds of kilowatts to me, and I immediately began to get itchy feet. My apprenticeship at Cammell Laird had finished in the power station, where I'd been involved in generating and transmitting power to the furnaces and throughout the works. Generation and power was in my blood, and at this time I was still really three-quarters transmitter-minded and only a quarter inclined towards outside broadcasting. So I wrote once more to the BBC chief engineer, Captain Eckersley, and asked for my name to be considered for a senior position.

One morning a letter arrived calling me to the BBC head office at Savoy Hill. They told me I should expect to stay a few weeks, so I found myself digs near Clapham Common. I went down in December 1924 and my time was spent assisting with the installation and layout of the headquarters control room, which incorporated the first simultaneous broadcast bay and GPO landline termination racks. Now we could switch rapidly from one to the other. It made it possible to accept programmes coming through the GPO landline from each of our regional stations and instantly switch over to transmission for broadcasting; and of course it allowed broadcast programmes to be sent instantly to the regions. Outside broadcasts also came to this unit through the GPO landline and could be transmitted immediately, and it gave us direct telephone contact between headquarters and any outside broadcast unit we set up. It was the most

May I Bring My Microphone?

impressive unit of its day.

After several weeks I got a new appointment, as senior engineer in charge of the experimental transmitter at Chelmsford. Here the brains of Marconi were constructing a 'lash-up' model, the test-bed of the design for a very high-powered transmitter that was to be built at Daventry. I went there after Christmas and found myself working alongside some of the most brilliant men in radio: Captain Round, Mr Ditcham, Mr Swann and Mr Tom Eckersley, the genius on the propagation of short-wave radio signals and brother of the BBC's chief engineer, Peter. There was a third, equally brilliant brother, Roger Eckersley, who eventually became head of programmes at the BBC.

My senior in the BBC at that time was Mr Litt, but he was occupied at the London office, and not in the best of health, and I saw little of him. I spent my time at Chelmsford, the nerve centre of radio equipment capable of enormous coverage. I was warned by everyone to be extremely careful because of the very high voltages being used, but the Marconi men, instead of taking care, took risks. Watching them move around with complete confidence while a thousand volts flew around in some places, you could see that they knew exactly what they were doing. These were the most knowledgeable and experienced men of their time in radio, and I sat at their feet and absorbed everything I could. They were a charming group: overnight they taught me, with no resentment or jealousy, things they had taken many years to learn.

A World in Your Ear

They were quick to notice any careless handling of equipment, knowing that in this situation a little knowledge could be truly dangerous, and that too many men were becoming radio experts overnight. The engineers at Marconi worked in specialized research groups, but nevertheless they all used to put their heads together at regular intervals to pool their achievements and discuss their projects, without fuss, pride or any attempt to impress falsely, or to hog their discoveries to themselves for their own advancement. They were developing the experimental basis of things to come, and what evolved became the 5XX long-wave transmitter of the BBC that was to open at Daventry in July 1925. It was a wonderful experience for me to meet the wizards of radio in this way, and I thought I had a job for life. I started negotiations for a small, Tudor-style house in Daventry and prepared to settle down.

But one day Captain Eckersley called me to Savoy Hill again and told me there was every likelihood of my being transferred to London, to pioneer outside broadcasts all over Britain. The change would come at short notice, he warned. I was not pleased at the idea, and asked if someone else could be considered in my place. But he refused to listen to my protests and painted a vivid picture of the work to be done. The BBC was going to bring famous dance bands to the nation; we were going to go into cathedrals and to the Lord Mayor's Banquets, to the Derby and the Boat Race. I would cover every national event, he promised. He did not mention wars, or abdications,

May I Bring My Microphone?

or kings. These were to come as a surprise to both of us. But I was warned that I should find myself accommodation within easy reach of the West End, the centre of entertainment, and bring all my ingenuity with me.

3

Baldwin and the Boat Race

So, in the spring of 1925 I went to live in London. What a change it was from Chelmsford. While I had been studying there with the Marconi team I had had fresh air, peace and quiet. Now I found myself in digs in Earl's Court Gardens, with breakfast and an evening meal provided at an exorbitant fee. I was told I had to live near the centre of town, for the keynote of my job was that I was to be handy, able as fast as possible to reach the studio or the outside venue from which we were broadcasting.

But no-one thought to arrange that I should receive more money to pay for my living in central London. The salary that had been comfortable in 1923 while I was living with my parents in the provinces went nowhere when I was on my own in the capital two years later. I often emptied my pockets out in the evening to find only pennies there, with not a shilling among them. Nor could I economize on clothes: the rule of the day with Reith and Eckersley was presentability. They would have had a fit if I had turned up in open-necked shirts or Oxford bags. When I went down on 23 November 1925 to arrange the opening of the new studio at Oxford University by Dr A.D.

Baldwin and the Boat Race

Lindsay, Master of Balliol, I naturally wore evening dress — and bought it myself.

I had arrived at the London office just as they were in the throes of covering the opening of the British Empire Exhibition at Wembley by King George V. It was the first-ever broadcast by a reigning British monarch, and many people recalled the historic occasion vividly even years later. In April 1964, for example, I got a letter from Sir Owen Morshead, librarian to the queen, commenting on my retirement, in which he wrote: 'If my memory is correct, I first heard "loud speaking" on the occasion of the opening of the great Wembley exhibition: I was walking down the street in Cambridge when there came blaring out of a shop doorway the voice of King George V.' People gathered together all over the country to listen to the broadcast and it was estimated that it was heard by over ten million people. We were becoming the enthusiasm of the majority.

We wanted to make daily broadcasts from the exhibition, and I had to put together a mobile transmission so that we could pick up interviews from different spots without trailing cables all over the exhibits. We built what we called a perambulator transmitter, a cumbersome thing carrying its own batteries, generators, microphone, amplifier and transmitter. We nicknamed this monster the 'coffin'; it moved around the exhibition, transmitting to a receiving point two or three hundred yards away for onward transmission by conventional landline. It gave us our first taste of flexibility. The 'coffin' was

A World in Your Ear

worked by a pioneer engineer called Mr Partridge, who had begun his radio career as a Marconi operator. He had the most amazing whistle — he could whistle the morse code much faster than anyone could tap it.

I was only too aware that we were going into the outside world without the necessary equipment. Everyone was keen to extend our horizons, and I was as enthusiastic as anyone. But when I look back, I marvel that we managed as we did. Our microphone then was the Marconi—Sykes magnetophone, a great square box covered with silk and known as the 'meatsafe'. This had to be polarized and supported in a rubber sling, and the moving coil within had to be suspended in position with cottonwool pads and adhesive. God help you if anyone opened a door suddenly and a gust of wind came by: it would blow the whole contraption out of use. The 'meatsafe' was also sufficiently magnetic to stop any watch that came too close, and the microphones in the studio carried a warning: 'If you cough or rustle your papers, you will deafen millions of listeners.'

It was this horror that I had to take down to Brighton, one day in the summer of 1925, for a hasty interview at the Metropole Hotel between Sir Harry Preston and the then undefeated American heavyweight boxer, Jack Dempsey. All the way there I worried in case the champion's voice proved to be as powerful as his fist, in which case it would certainly blow my microphone to pieces. But my concern was unnecessary, for he spoke as softly and gently as I could wish.

Baldwin and the Boat Race

Everything was happening within a matter of months. On 10 November 1925, the eve of Armistice Day, Edward, Prince of Wales, decided to broadcast a Poppy Day appeal. For this broadcast I managed to borrow two of the very newest Marconi–Reisz microphones. They consisted of a recessed block of marble only four inches square, with two spaced metal electrodes and a mica diaphragm filled with carbon granule dust. You had to shake the microphone just before you used it to loosen the granules and increase sensitivity. No stand had been provided to go with the new microphones and, as they had to be placed before the prince on the very ornate desk in his study at St James's Palace, I decided to do something about it. That night I took them back to my digs in Earl's Court and constructed two wooden bases which I painted with gold picture-frame lacquer. I thought they looked very elegant on his desk the next day.

By the end of that year I'd grown fed up with living alone in digs. I was busy working all over Christmas, and as soon as I had a few days leave accumulated in the new year, I went over to Bangor and asked Barbara to fix a wedding date quickly. Her parents agreed, I returned, and we married on 11 February in Bangor Abbey. J.C.W. Reith made us a personal wedding gift of ten guineas, and my colleagues presented us with a cased Crown Derby coffee set. But we came back to a small flat I'd rented in Manchester Street, just behind Selfridge's in London's Oxford Street. In those early days Reith would not allow his staff to buy houses, for he always felt the whole broadcasting venture was still too risky and uncertain for us to commit ourselves to financial burdens we would be unable to support if it collapsed.

I was once more under pressure to be handy, and this little flat was all I could find in a hurry. It was self-contained and furnished, with a bedroom, kitchen, bathroom and living room, and was admirably close to the BBC transmitter on Selfridges roof — but at 50 shillings a week, plus a meter for electricity, it swallowed two-thirds of my salary and we were almost penniless.

I had promised Barbara a honeymoon in Belgium in the spring, but we had hardly settled down in London when the General Strike happened. Those people who lived on the outskirts of London were told to stay at home: with no public transport they were stranded. But since I was unfortunate enough to live within walking distance of Savoy Hill I was expected to turn up, honeymoon or no honeymoon. It was 30 years before we finally got to Brussels, though by then we had been to many other places. And when we finally made it we both had the same thought, though we said nothing. We sat in the square in Brussels; I bought my wife a charm for her bracelet, and some cufflinks for myself, and we had a drink and said, 'And Brussels to you!'

Luckily Barbara has a great sense of humour, but it was a terrific shock to her to come from a big, friendly family in Northern Ireland to live alone in a tiny London flat with a husband who was out all the

Baldwin and the Boat Race

hours of the day. At the end of six months we moved out to Barons Court; again we felt we had to be near a tube station. So we took a three-year lease on a flat (in those days you had to take three-year agreements and you could not afford to break them).

The General Strike kept me frantically busy. But it also helped to bring home to people the importance of this new medium, the wireless. With no newspapers, and no contact with people through work to exchange news and gossip, radio became a very important way of letting people know what was happening. Reith suggested that it was an opportune time for the prime minister, Stanley Baldwin, to broadcast to the nation; and he agreed.

I was asked to install a duplicate set of outside broadcasting equipment in a convenient cupboard just outside the Cabinet Room at 10 Downing Street. We felt it best to have our own equipment there 'on site', so that, in an emergency, royalty or the prime minister could use it. But for Baldwin's broadcast, the first-ever by a British prime minister, we used our usual equipment. In the space of a year the British people had heard, live, the voices of the king, the Prince of Wales and the prime minister.

We were offering a unique and independent means of communication, and more and more ordinary people started to buy crystal or single-valve battery-operated receivers. As the General Strike continued, a police guard was mounted all around Savoy Hill and I had to make my way through it every morning.

But, with the ending of the strike and the slow

A World in Your Ear

return to normal, politics soon gave way to other things. We were starting to bring dance band after dance band on to the air. I was now able to use two or even three microphones for the unique sounds of the great big bands: Ambrose at the Mayfair Ballroom, the Savoy Hotel Orpheans with Carroll Gibbons, Geraldo, Harry Roy at the Cavour Restaurant, Leicester Square, and Billy Cotton playing in a club nearby. The Grand Hotel, Eastbourne, where Albert Sandler played on Sunday nights, was a real find — an acoustic gem; our research department carried out a big investigation to try and duplicate its acoustics elsewhere, but with only fair success. De Groot with his orchestra from the Piccadilly Hotel was a true perfectionist; so was a conductor who became a good friend of mine, Emilio Columbo, who played at the old Metropole and featured an up-and-coming violinist called Mantovani. In those days listeners could tell from the sound where the broadcast was coming from; we wanted to emphasize that this was no mere studio performance but a live band playing to a real audience in its usual surroundings.

To start with I had to make appointments with the various managements involved, to explain in detail once more what outside broadcasts were all about. Accommodation for the bulky battery-operated equipment and for an engineer had to be found; I had to arrange for the microphone to be suspended, or positioned on stands, and for cables to be laid to the control point, without spoiling the look of a luxurious hotel, or tripping up the waiters in a top-class

Baldwin and the Boat Race

restaurant. The GPO were again consulted, and they agreed to provide two circuits from the venue to the control room at Savoy Hill. One of these, the one with the best frequency range, was for the music, the other for telephone liaison and to be used in an emergency for the music if the first circuit failed. This cost money we scarcely had, and in each case we had to consider whether to rent accommodation on a daily, weekly, monthly or permanent basis, making guesses about how popular a certain band was likely to become. But we coped, and constantly extended our activities. The dear old 'coffin' transmitter, developed for the Wembley exhibition, proved its usefulness over and over again.

One popular outside broadcast location was London Zoo, where we did many relays for 'Children's Hour', narrated by David Seth-Smith the zooman. One of the funniest was in August 1926 when I decided to record the noises from the fish tank at suppertime. It was easy enough to run wires to the aquarium, for by this time several of the animal enclosures were permanently connected up to Savoy Hill. But how was I to construct an underwater microphone? In the end, since no hydrophone (the true underwater microphone) was available, I was forced to improvise. I took a telephone earpiece and wrapped its diaphragm in cotton wool and Vaseline. The whole was then put into a child's balloon, sealed up and lowered into the water on the end of a long bamboo pole.

The first sound we picked up was the splashing and

bubbling of the air inlet. Then we moved along the tank, and the large sea perch who shared the tank with the conger eels began to show a lively curiosity about the strange object, so we had to snatch it out of the water quickly. But eventually we were able to pick up the eerie sound of them smacking their jaws in noisy approval, the crunch of the crabs that they were eating for supper, and the sudden swish of water as the eels came nosing up.

This spurred us on to another underwater adventure. It was decided to put a diver into the Thames from the steps of County Hall. I made up another improvised hydrophone like the one we had used for the conger eels, and the diver spoke through this inside his glass helmet. But no-one had anticipated the results. The trouble was that he had only gone a few feet down when he found visibility going. The water was filthy, polluted and dead, and without flares he could see nothing — or, if he could, it was not fit to describe to the listeners' delicate sensibilities. The experiment ended quickly. But it had seemed like a good idea; we were ready to try anything.

I vividly remember, on a late June evening, watching and recording the spectacle of marching, music and searchlights that makes up the Aldershot Tattoo. The sight of the vehicles slowly disappearing into the surrounding woods, and the soldiers making their exit into the darkness as the searchlights dimmed and the band played *The Flowers of the Forest*, was unforgettable.

And, every New Year's eve in the late 1920s, there

was a most demanding outside broadcast called 'The Grand Goodnight', organized by the great J.C. Stobart. Programme contributions would be taken from Hilversum and other world-famous broadcasting centres, leading up to the final midnight blessing by the Archbishop of Canterbury from his stall in the choir of the empty and echoing Canterbury Cathedral. Well, not quite empty: I was there with my microphone.

Cathedrals were beginning to appear regularly in my schedule. We covered enthronements of the archbishops at Canterbury Cathedral and York Minster, and services from most of the other leading cathedrals, including Durham, Chester, Lincoln, Winchester, Chichester and Ely. One surprise came when I was asked to organize a broadcast on 18 October 1926 from the mighty organ of Liverpool Cathedral. This seemed like a fairly routine matter to me, until I arrived there and discovered that the cathedral was not yet built. The nave did not exist at all at that time, and halfway down the site there was a temporary brick wall cutting the completed part of the building off from the work still in progress. This wall played havoc with the acoustics; it took me three days and nights to obtain a satisfactory balance of sound. But I was helped enormously by the cathedral organist, Goss Custard, who played tirelessly for me by the hour while I disappeared into the roof to try various adjustments.

It was here that I first met Dean Dwelley, an outstanding man who became a good friend. He intro-

A World in Your Ear

duced me to Sir Giles Scott, the cathedral's architect, and on many occasions Sir Giles sought my advice about acoustic considerations involved in the construction of this great building. At J.C.W. Reith's direction I also acted as consultant to Sir Edward Maufe, architect of Guildford Cathedral, over acoustical problems there. Little by little I built up a set of plans of all Britain's great cathedrals, with my own notes on their acoustics and facilities, which I kept in my office. Cathedrals have the supreme advantage of not changing their acoustics, unlike open-air events such as the Aldershot Tattoo, and it would be as easy to plan a cathedral broadcast from my schemes today as it was then.

The only challenge I turned down in those tumultuous days was an offer made early in 1926 to become chief engineer of the new Indian Broadcasting Company which was just being established. The starting salary was the enormous sum of £1000 a year, with an annual increment of £250. The conditions and contract seemed like a rajah's ransom. But I could not make up my mind, nor would Barbara or my parents offer me any encouragement. I was afraid the company might collapse, leaving me high and dry, whereas the BBC now looked set to survive after its cliff-hanging start. In the end I turned the offer down. The Bombay station was eventually opened in July 1929 by the Viceroy of India, Lord Irwin. The BBC relayed the ceremony. What a fool I was!

We were now getting more cooperation from

theatre managers, who had been among the most hostile opponents of radio at the start, so that we were able to broadcast plays as well as music. One early successs was the relaying of a whole act of *Yvonne* from the stage of Daly's Theatre, Leicester Square (now the Warner cinema). It starred Gene Gerrard and Ivy Tresmand, who I thought was stunning, and was staged by a famous owner—director, Jimmy White. Our outside broadcast unit had to be accommodated in the orchestra pit. Later on, when we went into theatres, we were promoted to the side of the stage, or a convenient corner of a dressing room or green room if one existed.

There were more adventurous appointments to keep too. I remember in October 1926 being on the terrace of the Houses of Parliament, jostled by cabinet ministers and other VIPs, while we all awaited the arrival of Sir Alan Cobham, who had just flown solo from Australia via Cape Town. He flew nonchalantly down the Thames, sweeping under the bridge in his tiny flying boat and finally touching down on the river right in front of us. He climbed out of the cockpit into a small launch, surrounded by river police to keep away the crowds, and came ashore on to the terrace where Gerald Cock interviewed him.

In September 1926 I applied for membership of the Institute of Radio Engineers in New York. I had become increasingly aware of the fact that they catered more fully for the requirements of broadcasting and its equipment than our Institute of

A World in Your Ear

Electrical Engineers. I was accepted into full membership although I was still only 23, and celebrated with an experiment I had been longing to try for some time: the world's first-ever stereo broadcast.

I approached Captain Eckersley and the head of our development department, Captain West, with the suggestion that I should attempt a two-channel transmission of an opera from the Old Vic theatre. This meant renting two music circuits and a third control circuit. One music circuit would be connected to the 5XX station at Daventry and the other to the London 2LO transmitter on the roof of Selfridge's. The third was the usual control circuit and led to Savoy Hill.

My superiors were a bit dubious about the extra expense involved in renting a third circuit, but it was eventually agreed to, and a handful of people were provided with receivers: one headphone for the 5XX transmission, the other for the 2LO transmission. Reception was excellent, and on that day in 1926 live stereophonic broadcasting was born. Unfortunately it also died again, for there was no money available for me to pursue any further experiments in stereo transmission. Ironically, I was asked to broadcast my reminiscences of this landmark on the BBC Third Programme 40 years later, on 3 October 1964, and was paid seven guineas. This sum of money, if it had been available in 1926, would have paid for the complete experiment — and allowed me to take out patent rights as well.

At the end of 1927 we made a broadcast from the Tower of London that was to set a pattern of

Baldwin and the Boat Race

precision timing and accurate microphone mixing. Our aim was to cover the daily Ceremony of the Keys there. This is the traditional locking-up of the Tower each night which has been enacted daily for some 700 years. The origin of the ceremony probably lies in the fact that the great Norman fortress was used not only as a royal residence, but also as the home of the Mint and the crown jewels, and as the state prison. In the days when the king could not count on the enthusiasm of the people of London, who might have designs on his money or sympathy for his prisoners, it was essential to make sure the Tower was absolutely secure. So the chief warder would go round every night with an armed escort, locking all the gates and doors, and then hand the keys over to the governor for the night.

The ceremony starts at exactly 9.53 each night, the chief warder following a prescribed route as he does his rounds. To give a true picture of it meant wiring up the various points on the route and switching from one to the next at just the right moment. Without TV monitor screens, or even two-way talk-back facilities, only luck and split-second timing enabled us to switch over at precisely the right moment to the next microphone in sequence. But despite my palpitations the broadcast was so successful that it was repeated many times, and HMV made a record of it that was very popular and sold worldwide.

The BBC reached another milestone in 1927, for on 1 January of that year the British Broadcasting

A World in Your Ear

Corporation took over the duties and responsibilities of the company. We were now firmly established: over two million people held wireless licences and our total audience numbered millions more. We had brought radio to theatres and schools, churches and factories, we had put politicians and kings, sportsmen and entertainers in front of the microphone, and we had made listening to the radio an essential and familiar part of British life. There was still no pension scheme at the BBC, but it was on its way. For no-one could argue now that radio had no future. The new corporation was ready to expand in all sorts of new directions, and one of the first was sport.

Until 1926 the GPO had given in to pressure from the press not to allow the BBC to compete with news presentation, even of sporting news. But now the ban was lifted. So on 15 January I found myself sitting in a prefabricated hut controlling the first outside broadcast of a rugby match from Twickenham. Later we were to get a fully equipped outside broadcast van and a permanent box in the main grandstand, but at that time our equipment was housed in an ordinary van parked nearby. The commentator was Captain Teddy Wakelam, and the teams were England and Wales, but I don't recall who won. I never had much time for sport as a boy. I don't believe I have played above three games of football in my life. And though I did promise to turn out for the BBC cricket team once or twice, in the early days when the staff was so small that they would use almost anybody, I almost always had to cancel because some broadcasting commitment would come up. We are a most unsporting family, except for my wife who, like her father, is a fine rifle shot.

My work was taking me to some pretty unusual places. Soon after the broadcast from Twickenham, I found myself in a Surrey wood in the middle of the night. I was not the only strange visitor. With me was the celebrated cellist, Beatrice Harrison, sitting unperturbed in a clearing playing her instrument. The object was to tempt the nightingales to sing so that I could capture their song. We had to use the cumbersome magnetophone microphone to keep down the noise level and improve the quality, but its delicate suspension meant it was upset by any sudden gust of wind. It was not the ideal equipment for an outdoor broadcast at midnight. But the nightingales were duly captivated by the glorious music of the cello, and we soon became expert at capturing their song unless the wind 'blew it' for us.

In that year of 1927 the landmarks in outside broadcasting came so thick and fast that I scarcely had time to agonize over the chance of anything going wrong; I was too busy with the next 'impossible' assignment. The first broadcast from Twickenham in January was followed by the first live commentary on the Grand National on 25 March.

The BBC had made one or two approaches to Mrs Mirabelle Topham, who owned the Aintree racecourse, but she had always refused permission for us to broadcast the race. In the end Reith asked me if I would go up and try my luck, since by then I had more experience than most in introducing the idea of broadcasting to reluctant strangers. I walked all round the famous course with her — she was a friendly, lively person, immensely proud of the great race and eager to talk about it. Then she asked if I would like a drink, and we went back and had a few. And whether it was because I had shown a genuine interest in her beloved National, because I talked to her with my usual passionate fervour about the importance of broadcasting (for there was no believer more enthusiastic than me), or because I matched her drink for drink, I don't know, but eventually she agreed that I could attempt a broadcast.

It had to be transmitted worldwide, for there was considerable overseas interest in the race, especially in America. Hundreds of Americans used to come over for it. They would charter a liner and sail over, berth in the Mersey and live on board, coming ashore for the racing.

I spent some time up at Aintree before the race, pacing round the course and calculating where to place my microphones — both for the commentators, and in order to capture the atmosphere in the winners' unsaddling enclosure. On the day of the race I had a thousand things on my mind, and failed to pay proper attention when the commentator, Mr Meyrick Good, came up to me beforehand with the tip of a certainty he'd been given. I had no time to place a bet, and was really too preoccupied to think of it. But the broadcast went off without a hitch. Half an hour after the race I felt a tap on my shoulder.

Baldwin and the Boat Race

'Did you bet on that horse I told you?' demanded Meyrick Good. I had to confess that I had not. He called me a few names, because the horse had indeed won. Then he smiled and pressed some crisp pound notes into my hand. 'I knew you wouldn't have time, so I did it for you,' he said. A great broadcaster and a great gentleman, he was the commentator for the first two Grand Nationals.

I was learning that an outside broadcast engineer must have zest for the job and some flair with his hands; book knowledge was not enough — it was all improvisation. When you are alone in the middle of Salisbury Plain with a military tattoo on, you have got to make it work. You cannot hope to ring up and say, 'Please take over or put a recording on.' The Grand National is only run once.

One week after that first Grand National broadcast I was up to my neck in the watery problems of our first Oxford and Cambridge Boat Race. This was always one of the most difficult outside broadcasts of all, and one of the coldest and most miserable. The problem was that there was no chance of a telephone link to the control room at Broadcasting House to check if our signals were being received. We had to do it all by timing, and trust that it would all run smoothly.

So out came the old 'coffin' once more, the mobile transmitter that had been used for the Wembley exhibition and London Zoo. I had it rebuilt and modified: the amplifiers, motor generator and accumulators had to be installed and set up on sponge rubber to avoid vibration from the boat's engine. A special shield was built around the microphone to guard against wind, rain and spray, and this had to be watched to see that it did not deaden the voice or give too much of an echo. Then all the equipment was fitted into the hired launch *Magician* for the maiden voyage down the Thames. There were various technical problems; the chief one was the limit on the height of our aerial, which had to be low enough to pass safely beneath the bridges. Beneath the bridges the commentator, too, had to learn to raise his voice, as the sound would otherwise fade away.

We had only one channel, which carried the broadcast from the boat for transmission, so there was no feedback to enable you to listen to how things were going; it was all done blind. I began two days before the race, setting up a reception point, for the transmission from the launch, on the roof of the Harrods furniture depository by the side of the river halfway down the course. On the day itself we took up position, cramped into the *Magician*, with the 'coffin' itself taking up most of the space and the commentators and I balancing where we could. We had to hold our launch behind the Oxford and Cambridge boats and the umpire's. There is a lot of ceremony before the race begins, and we were afraid of getting left behind as it started, or going too fast in our powered launch and upsetting the competitors in our wash. All the time I was searching among the thousands of people in the crowd along the banks for a man waving a handkerchief to tell us our signal was

Baldwin and the Boat Race

getting through successfully.

The commentator for the first two Boat Races was Gully Nickalls, helped on the first occasion by Sir John Squire. Nickalls had rowed three times in the Oxford crew himself, was twice a silver medallist in the Olympics and later president of the Leander rowing club at Henley, chairman of the Amateur Rowing Association and senior steward of Henley Royal Regatta. He gave a uniquely well-informed and interesting description of the event to the thousands of listeners who were hearing about it for the first time.

The commentator disembarked at the finishing-point at Barnes and we sailed back to the boathouse at St Margaret's, further up the river. There I finally managed to find a telephone. It had taken time to unload our gear, and not until a couple of hours after the race was I able to ask the control room at Savoy Hill, 'How did the Boat Race go?' The engineer said 'Wait a minute, sir,' and consulted his log book. I was told it had gone off fine.

We now had the sporting bit between our teeth. Enthusiasts of every sort wanted to hear their favourite sport on the air and we tried radio coverage of them all. We did snooker from Leicester Square, for instance. We had a good commentator, and you could hear the tap of the billiard balls. As long as the commentator knew what he was talking about you could convey a lot. In the early days of football we used to print a diagram of the pitch in *Radio Times* marked out in squares, and he could explain that a

A World in Your Ear

certain player was in a particular square.

The first regular Saturday football commentary was from a little wooden hut at the side of Crystal Palace's pitch; the commentator was George Allison, a director of Arsenal and pioneer of commentary who had a remarkable, deep-toned broadcasting voice. He was always sure of his facts, with an enviable capacity to comment succinctly on the team's successes and failures. He was rather a large gentleman, and it was said of him that his dimensions extended chiefly sideways. I arranged the first live broadcast of the Association Football Cup Final at Wembley on 23 April 1927, providing clean sound into a number of different circuits for all the overseas commentators who used to cover the Cup Final in those days.

As the summer of 1927 grew near I began negotiations with Major D.R. Larcombe, secretary of the All England Club, for permission to broadcast from Wimbledon. After much discussion he finally agreed. A permanent soundproof hut was built for the commentator on staging at the side of the court, wired to a control point underneath the terraces. The first live coverage of the famous lawn tennis championships took place on 2 July. The hut I built is still there, now joined by others for the television services.

That summer of 1927 also saw the first live commentary on the Derby (on 1 June), on the Lincoln and on cricket from Lords and the Oval, and coverage of the TT motorcycle races from the Isle of Man. This last venue brought back many happy memories for me, and I was delighted return there.

Baldwin and the Boat Race

One of the fascinations of outside broadcasting for me was its absolute unpredictability. Other men in the BBC might be typecast into 'sports' or 'variety' or 'talks', but I moved from one world to another wherever a live microphone was needed outside the studio walls, and I saw the great affairs of state in close-up, as well as the pleasures of the people.

In 1927 I arranged broadcast coverage of the ceremonial state funerals of Admiral of the Fleet Lord Jellicoe and Earl Beatty. All their lives they had been at loggerheads, but they were buried side by side at St Paul's Cathedral. The first broadcast from the Whitehall Cenotaph took place that year too. The occasion was a British Legion Memorial Service, the forerunner of the 11 November Armistice Day ceremony. I had to prepare a very detailed scale plan for approval by a select government committee headed by the prime minister, Stanley Baldwin. I drew on my experience in Manchester in deciding where I needed to site the microphones; I put one near the speakers, one near the bands and one at the Cenotaph itself to catch the rustle as the wreaths were laid down.

On 24 July I travelled to Belgium to cover another harrowing state occasion, the unveiling of the new memorial arch at the Menin Gate, Ypres, by Field-Marshal Lord Plumer, to mark the site where thousands of British and Allied troops had fallen in the 1914–18 war. At first the Imperial War Graves Commission had tried to bury the dead in individual graves, and 750,000 standard tombstones had been shipped over to Europe. But even these could not accommodate the half a million men unaccounted for, and at Menin, Blomfield the architect allowed room for 57,000 of what he called 'those intolerable nameless names' to be inscribed. That was not enough, either.

The Belgian telephone service was most cooperative and I was able to establish a landline between Ypres and London for the broadcast. King Leopold of the Belgians made a speech at the opening ceremony, and the transmission was one of the most memorable I had been involved in. Being able to listen to what was taking place at Ypres was a great comfort to the next of kin of the thousands who had died on this grim battlefield. I found myself very moved by the senseless loss of life, and still think about it to this day.

I travelled straight from Ypres to Dover and then to Ireland, as my wife was visiting her family and I wanted to have a few days' leave with her there. We were still living in our Barons Court maisonette and Barbara was expecting our first child, William Henry, who was born in London on 8 September 1927. Barons Court was not a very happy place to bring up a baby: there were incessant noise and fumes from the traffic, which we seemed unable to escape, and when our lease finally expired we seized the chance to move further out of London, to another maisonette in Streatham. Soon our daughter, Patricia, was born at my wife's home in Bangor on 12 February 1929.

On 28 August a second broadcast from Belgium followed the one from the Menin Gate. A cinema

Baldwin and the Boat Race

organ and dance band recital was relayed from the Kursaal d'Ostende, the entertainment centre of Ostend. Once again all the bulky battery-powered equipment had to be transported across from London in specially constructed tough wooden packing cases, and assembled when we got there for this precursor of the Eurovision Song Contest.

About this time I was asked by the head of outside broadcasts, Roger Eckersley, if I would help a friend of his with his radio equipment. It turned out to be George Black, managing director of a theatrical empire which included the Palladium and the Holborn Empire. He was in the habit, when he arrived home around midnight at the end of his working day, of spending some time before bed listening to short-wave broadcasts. He had mentioned his hobby, and the difficulty he was having adjusting his set accurately, to Mr Eckersley who at that time was most anxious to start broadcasting from some of the famous variety shows being put on at George Black's theatres. Although by now we were broadcasting concerts and plays quite frequently, the variety managers were the last to be persuaded of the need to cooperate with radio. Most of them feared it would kill their business, and many insisted on artists signing contracts which forbade them to appear on radio while the contract lasted. Mr Eckersley thought it was sensible to help George Black in any way we could, to show our good faith.

So I set off one evening for his house in Merton, Surrey (a stone's throw from where I now live) with

A World in Your Ear

orders to 'put him on the right lines' over his receiver and aerial system for long-distance short-wave reception. Black, always known in the theatre as 'The Guv'nor', was a charming man, and very grateful to me for my help. Soon we were relaying live variety shows from his theatres, and later the Royal Command Performance, complete with commentator, was broadcast from the stage of the Palladium. He used to direct the shows himself, looking like Al Capone in a trilby hat with the brim snapped down, and always with a cigar in his mouth. Whenever I appeared on the stage of the Palladium he would call a break saying, 'He's here again, girls, take five minutes.' Then, turning to me, he would ask patiently, 'Now, Woody, what can I do for you today?'

The first three or four Royal Command Performances were broadcast live, but as recording techniques improved we began to record and edit them for broadcasting later. All these early recordings were made on disc, of course, until after the end of World War II, when captured German equipment showed that they had developed magnetic tape and British and American manufacturers began to copy it. But in the 1920s we were working with pure ebonite discs. You could edit them by cutting into them, but it was hard work with all the swarf coming up. Later we began to use composition discs, and we could make a master disc and then record that on to other matrixes for editing on a hand-cutting machine. We had a groove counter, which enabled a needle to drop down automatically at the right place, but we also

Baldwin and the Boat Race

used our hands; it was something to see perhaps six different turntables going, with a hand or an automatic drop on each, chalk sections on the record indicating when to put in certain effects or speeches, and the whole then transferred on to a master. We managed pretty well.

By the end of 1927 we were carrying out one-hour outside broadcasts called 'seaside nights' from places like Margate and Eastbourne, and local entertainment from county towns such as Tunbridge Wells. These one-night stands were very popular, but they strained our resources, technical and physical, to the limit. For some time I had been planning a specially constructed control van, to make our work much easier. In the spring of 1928 our first purpose-built outside broadcast van took to the road. It was used for the first time at Bisley. The roof was reinforced to carry, if necessary, a prefabricated hut which could be erected hastily on site to protect the commentators from the weather and cut out unwanted noise.

In 1929 came a landmark in sound: the arrival of the talking picture. Sound of course made all the difference, for once those silent lips could speak, the films really sprang to life. And to anyone who thinks that pictures are more important than words, I would say that today you have millions of people who still find time to listen to the radio, even though it has no pictures, but no-one today is making silent films; for pictures without sound have no appeal.

In the autumn of 1929 the head of programmes at

A World in Your Ear

the BBC asked me if I could attempt to take an excerpt from the soundtrack of a film for broadcasting. We chose as our subject *The Love Parade*, a glamorous film starring Maurice Chevalier. I worked in a specially equipped Wardour Street studio at a private screening. I was greatly helped by some RCA engineers from America who were busy installing the first 'talkie' equipment into leading cinemas throughout Britain (all the installations were American at that time). Making full use of their experimental equipment, I managed to capture the excerpt successfully after a period of trial and error.

The arrival of sound had a big impact on cinema design. The old tin buildings had to be adapted and, with new cinemas varying considerably in design springing up everywhere, careful attention had to be paid to the acoustics every time we made an outside broadcast from a cinema. Today the same cinemas are being demolished or converted.

While I was down in Bournemouth one day, supervising the sound balance for the first broadcast of a super new cinema organ, I met the same team of RCA specialist engineers who had helped me with the first movie extract; they were installing complex talkie equipment in the cinema. They made me a tempting offer to join their business, but by now I was wedded to the BBC. However, there were very few engineers in Britain at that time with outside broadcast experience or knowledge of microphone technique and camouflage, so the arrival of the talkies meant I lost many of my most experienced staff to

Baldwin and the Boat Race

various film studios, at enhanced salaries. One eventual result was a slight uplift in the salaries of those loyal engineers who remained; so I, too, owed something to the advent of the talkies.

In April 1930 there came another request for a bit of private assistance to a radio enthusiast in trouble — this time from the director-general, now Sir John Reith. The enthusiast was Lord Beaverbrook, whose personal radiogram was proving difficult to adjust. It was arranged that his car would pick me up from Streatham Hill in the evening to take me down to his country home in Leatherhead, Surrey. So, after work, we motored down. But when I arrived on the doorstep, a valet opened the door and informed me that the eminent gentleman was not at home and would I take myself round to the tradesmen's entrance?

I turned on my heel, got back into the chauffeur-driven saloon and told the driver to take me and my testing equipment back to Streatham immediately. First thing the next morning, Sir John telephoned me in my office to ask how things had gone. I told him, and he was very cross; for to him a slight to his staff was a slur on the whole BBC. But another date was made for the following evening. This time Lord Beaverbrook himself opened the door and escorted me into the enormous dining room where he showed me the largest radiogram I had ever seen. I was amused to see that this advocate of empire free trade, whose newspaper the *Daily Express* regularly exhorted its readers to buy only from countries in the British Empire, had bought his own radiogram

A World in Your Ear

from the Radio Corporation of America. He explained that his son Max had got things a trifle tangled up: the auto-changer was jammed, the turning mechanism was adrift and the whole system was out of balance.

It took me a few hours to put the whole thing right, watched by Lord Beaverbrook and his butler, who had come in with his throat spray. Then the car whisked me home again near midnight, and I reported next day to Sir John that the mission was complete. I also had a letter that day from Lord Beaverbrook thanking me. Sir John appreciated my help: he thought at that time that Beaverbrook was likely to assume some major importance in British affairs and that it was sensible to keep in favour with him.

Late in 1932 I again had to think seriously about my future when I was offered the job of assistant superintendent engineer of the BBC in Scotland. But once more the offer came at the wrong time. I had just, at last, started to buy a house of my own in the leafy suburb of Merton. It had a garden for the children and for me. Unlike my father (I've never met a journalist yet who could tell a flower from a weed) I was keen on my gardening, even though much of it was done by candlelight when I got home. After years of being too available to the BBC, I was beginning to enjoy a home life of my own at last, and to see a little of my growing children. I hesitated to move to Glasgow. It was easier to buy a house than to sell one in those Depression years: I was afraid I would not get a decent price for mine. Besides, we would have had to move at our own expense, since there were no

Baldwin and the Boat Race

transfer allowances or bridging loans available in those days to staff on the move. So I turned it down and stayed in London with a life that, had I known it, was going to become far more hectic than I could imagine.

In February 1934 I undertook to make a 'sound picture' of the opening of Battersea Power Station, one of our most ambitious undertakings yet. This was the very latest in high-power generation, and I remembered my own apprentice days at Cammell Laird as I toured the works hunting for places to site my microphones. I used nine, each insulated so as to receive its own sound and no other, and with the commentator Howard Marshall we were able to illustrate the whole system — the coal being taken to the furnaces, the steam to the turbines, the electricity from the generators to the switching chambers. Different microphones caught the hum of the turbines and generators, the throbbing of the massive circulating pumps (each handling two and a quarter million gallons of Thames water an hour for the cooling system), the sound of the contact arm of one of the main switches going into commission, and finally the hum of the great transformers which are coupled to the grid network at 132,000 volts.

This was the best sort of outside broadcast — carefully planned for the finest possible result; but we seldom had time for that sort of organization. More typical was one of the most exciting broadcasts of the year, which we did when a great fire broke out at the rubber warehouse near Wapping police station

A World in Your Ear

on the north side of the Thames. It burnt fiercely for many days and I was asked if it would be possible to set up a live 'description of the scene' (the word 'commentary' had still to come into use). A.P. Herbert's barge *The Water Lily* came to my rescue. We managed to load on board the cumbersome equipment we needed, including the enormous outside broadcast transmitter and accumulators, and reception points were established on a warehouse roof and at the police station.

The splendidly-named Commander Firebrace, a senior officer of the London Fire Brigade, and his men at Wapping gave us all their help, and the commentary was given by Commander Borritt and his wife, Sheila. We had to manage as usual with only one-way transmission. But we chose a dark evening, and a torch waved by an assistant acted as a sufficient signal to 'go ahead' and 'finish'. During the whole of the broadcast one of my hands was on the controls, the other on my heart; but, amazingly, it all worked.

I had my next encounter with royalty in September 1934, when Queen Mary launched the giant liner number 534 (the 534th ship to be built at the Clydebank yards of John Brown), soon to become world famous as the *Queen Mary*. Unlike the king, who had a rather guttural accent, Queen Mary had a good broadcasting voice. But she was simply not interested in the medium, and made only one or two broadcasts in her life (the other broadcast of hers that I covered was when she opened the new YWCA building in Great Russell Street, London).

Baldwin and the Boat Race

I used 13 microphones altogether to cover the launch — my requirements were going up with each new challenge: two for the king, one each for the queen, Sir Percy Bates (chairman of Cunard and a great personal friend of Sir John Reith) and the christening bottle, three for the commentator, two for the slipway effects, two for the band and one more for water effects. They all had to be protected from the weather and from crowd movements in the dockyard, and those used for the tidal effects were, as before, placed in rubber balloons. 13 must have been my lucky number that day, for the broadcast went off without a hitch, and I returned to the *Queen Mary* a year later for one of the most testing and exhilarating enterprises of my life.

By the end of 1934 we were beginning to flex our muscles. We had been broadcasting for ten years now and there was no longer any doubt that we were there to stay. We had covered entertainment and sport, politics and news events, and now we were to embark on one of our most ambitious broadcasting projects yet.

The Duke of Kent had become the envy of everyone by his engagement to Princess Marina, one of the most beautiful women of her generation. He was to be married on 29 November 1934 in Westminster Abbey, and Sir John Reith at once began trying to persuade the prime minister and parliament to allow us to broadcast the whole ceremony. To my surprise, and a little to my dismay, permission was given for what I knew would be an incredibly demanding task.

A World in Your Ear

I set to work two months before the event, planning in detail the placing of my microphones. We wanted to capture the whole event from the moment the bride entered the church, which presented the technical problem of placing microphones in a line down the whole length of the abbey from the great west door to the altar, with additional ones near the bells, the choir, the organ and the commentator outside. It was one thing to decide where I wanted to put them, however, and quite a different thing to find a suitable spot. For no-one, least of all myself, wanted ugly microphones and cables to spoil the appearance of the abbey on this happy occasion. So I hunted out hiding places, secreting them behind pillars, under statues, beneath chairs and behind candles. Without damaging the priceless fabric of the ancient abbey, we had to loop our hundreds of yards of cable back to a tiny control room that had been contrived for me in a small room in the crypt, just a few feet away from the Tomb of the Unknown Warrior.

This was the most difficult of the 13,000 outside broadcasts we had made. For two months I paced the floor of the abbey, timing the service and the procession, testing placings and trying to balance the mix of sound coming through. For, as I switched from one microphone to the next as the bride walked down the aisle, and switched over to the choir, the organ or the archbishop's microphone at the appropriate moment, I had to be sure there was no awkward jarring of sound, and had to keep the level absolutely constant so that the organ did not drown the choir or the listener feel he had 'jumped' from one spot to another. And, once again, it all had to be done quite blind, for I could not see into the abbey from my control room. For over four hours I sat at the controls and simply had to hope that my timing and preparations were exact, and that all the parties concerned were in fact standing where I had estimated they would be when I switched from microphone to microphone.

My greatest fear was over the microphone I had suspended only three feet above the heads of the bride and groom to catch each all-important 'I will', the most vital part of the ceremony. At this point I turned my amplifier control switch to maximum to catch the murmured responses. Heaven help me if anyone had sneezed, or knocked over a chair in the nave in their keenness to get a better view: many transmitters would have been overloaded and would have flashed over and off the air; overload safety switches would have come into operation and closed them down. So I crossed my fingers, held my breath and waited. It was all right. The responses were duly recorded, I lowered the volume to a safer level once more, and the service proceeded smoothly and joyously to its conclusion.

The commentator before and after the service (we did not have one inside the abbey itself) was Howard Marshall. He was sitting on the roof of the Westminster Hospital nearby in a portable outside broadcast commentary hut we had now developed;

A World in Your Ear

it had acoustic walls to give good speech reproduction, sliding glass windows, and even a cushioned seat — altogether superior to the early facilities we had had to make do with. Marshall described the arrival of the guests, headed by the king and queen who were followed by the Duke of Kent, the Prince of Wales who was best man, the other royal guests, and finally Princess Marina and her bridesmaids. He was a marvellous commentator on ceremonial occasions, knowledgeable and fluent. The service was relayed to Italy, Yugoslavia, Denmark, Holland, Germany, Austria and the two national broadcasting systems of America. With the exception of King George V's Christmas Day broadcasts from Sandringham this royal wedding had the biggest worldwide listening audience of any transmission so far.

Soon after the event, the director-general presented me with a specially boxed set of records covering the whole service, which I still have. Inside the lid was his own note saying 'R.H. Wood: a fine act magnificently carried out.' Typically of Reith, the note was in Latin. Soon afterwards a senior engineer called me into his office and handed me a soiled envelope, explaining that he had been carrying it around and forgotten to give it to me. Inside was a £15 bonus from Sir John, who did not hand out cheques lightly, but whose personal interest in the day-to-day operations of the BBC in every sphere was phenomenal.

The success of the broadcast showed the royal family that the BBC could handle great occasions unobtrusively and well, and that the whole world would listen. It was a success that was to lead directly to the broadcasting of the next coronation.

The next year, 1935, was crowded with royal events. King George's health was rumoured to be failing, but plans pushed ahead to make this a jubilee year marking his 25 years on the throne. The jubilee thanksgiving service was held on a wonderful sunny day in early May at St Paul's Cathedral. I decided to try and capture the flavour of the celebrations throughout the procession, and set up microphones along Temple Bar, down Fleet Street, through Ludgate Circus and up Ludgate Hill to St Paul's. Microphones to pick up street noises were concealed in the statue of a griffin that stands in Fleet Street and on the railway bridge over Ludgate Hill, and we managed to pick up the voice of London — not just the bells pealing from hundreds of church towers, but the noises of the crowd, the cheering and the singing — to make a most vivid background to the commentary.

I used 27 microphones altogether, with three control points: one was in a flat borrowed from a kindly gentleman whose rooms happened to overlook Temple Bar, another near Ludgate railway bridge, and the main control room was inside St Paul's. There were four commentators this time including Howard Marshall, who described the procession along the route, and Stephen King-Hall, who was positioned above the great door in the western façade of the cathedral to cover the service. The Duchess of Kent won the loudest cheers as she went by in an open carriage, holding down a large-brimmed hat with one hand and waving with the other, looking every inch the ideal of a fairytale princess.

By now I had been given a secretary: 11 years after I had joined the BBC, someone had finally noticed how busy I was. And soon after that, in true bureaucratic tradition, I was given an office junior as well. I needed them both, for I was working furiously. In that jubilee year we covered, for the first time, the army review at Aldershot and the naval review at Spithead. Of course the latter, on 16 July 1935, the first-ever broadcast from a battleship, was the most difficult.

I had to install a miniature broadcasting station on the battleship *Royal Sovereign*, so out once more came the 'coffin' transmitter, veteran of the Wembley Exhibition and now stalwart of the Boat Race. We fitted it into the dentist's cabin, and hoped no-one would get toothache for a few days. Microphones were placed all over the ship and an aerial was slung between a disused observation tower on shore and a nearby lighthouse. To receive our signals, two special receivers (one a spare in case the other failed) were fitted into the military observation tower of Southsea Castle at Portsmouth and from there the broadcasts were relayed by GPO landline all the way to Broadcasting House in London. We had to take care not to interfere with the *Royal Sovereign's* normal radio service, and a secret wavelength was used for our link with Southsea Castle. The guest of honour on board the *Royal Sovereign* was the Rt Hon. Ramsay MacDonald, one of the rare politicians who showed

Baldwin and the Boat Race

great interest in what I was doing.

Working with the navy brought me one great advantage: although we still had no means of setting up a two-way radio link, the naval command did place at my disposal two radio officers, Commander Harper and Commander Robinson from *HMS Collingwood*, the navy's radio-telephony headquarters. These two splendid fellows laid on a two-way link for me, using heliograph and searchlight morse, and it worked admirably. Having often sat at my lonely controls in the middle of the Thames or on the plains at Aldershot, wishing fervently that I had some sort of Red Indian smoke signal for sending messages by, I very much appreciated this help.

Thanks to all the cooperation from the Royal Navy it all went off smoothly. Listeners heard the thunder of the royal salute, the ship's bugles, the boatswain's pipes, the ship's bands and all the cheering. Radio was used to synchronize the firing of the royal salute and the firework display by the 150 vessels of the fleet which were 'in line' for the review.

I carried out my last Christmas Day broadcast with George V at Sandringham at the end of that jubilee year. A month later, at the age of 70, he died, and his body lay in state in Westminster Hall before the burial at Windsor Castle. The BBC made arrangements to cover the whole funeral ceremony, which involved detailed coverage from Westminster Hall, from Paddington Station where the coffin and the chief mourners were to board a train for Windsor, of the arrival at Windsor Station and of the gun carriage

A World in Your Ear

procession to St George's Chapel at Windsor Castle.

We decided early on that a commentary would be superfluous and intrusive, so the whole picture of the event was conveyed by pure sound: the rhythmic steps as the gun carriage carrying the king's coffin, manned by Royal Navy ratings, was pulled step by slow step along the winding road to Windsor Castle, the muted commands, the tolling bells and the muffled gun salutes. The broadcast went out all over the world and in my opinion was one of the finest sound portrayals we ever achieved. Like the jubilee day service from St Paul's, the funeral was heard by a very high proportion of the people of Britain listening in together and sharing their feelings in a way that was unknown before radio brought together all the individuals at home into one united audience.

On 20 January 1936 I supervised the simple broadcast, from the balcony overlooking the forecourt of St James's Palace, of the proclamation of King Edward VIII as King-Emperor. Behind an upstairs window was Mrs Simpson, though none of us then realized how significant this was.

As 1935 turned into 1936, the most exciting thing in my life was the knowledge that I was to sail on the maiden voyage of the *Queen Mary* to New York, arranging live broadcasts during the crossing. From December 1935 onwards I began to make regular trips to Glasgow, travelling up one night and down the next, to decide on the siting of the various microphones and the control point. I decided to install 29 microphone points at places that varied from the

Baldwin and the Boat Race

crow's nest to the swimming pool, by way of the dining room, ballroom, sun decks, embarkation decks and engine room, so that listeners could be taken on a complete tour of the ship by radio. The installation and routing of the miles of wire needed for the microphone circuits was carried out under my supervision by the shipbuilders, John Brown, for the wires had to be hidden behind the panels before the ship was finally fitted out and painted. By the great liner's maiden voyage, on 27 May 1936, she had become a floating broadcasting centre. Just to walk round and say 'Can you hear me?' into each microphone point for checking took one of my engineers over four hours.

I was allocated a marvellous suite on the sun deck, and thought the trip was going to be a real break for me after all the months of preparation (though we sailed on Derby day, which put something of a strain on the outside broadcasting unit). The BBC team on board numbered nine. There was the Glasgow novelist and journalist George Blake, the assistant controller of programmes Roger Eckersley, the commentator John Snagge, the radio producer John Watt and his secretary Celia Cushion, myself and three assistant engineers, C.M. Hall, J.P. Howard and W.G. Preston. Henry Hall the bandleader was there too, to entertain the passengers, as was the up-and-coming Larry Adler. George Blake covered the ship's departure from Southampton, and also did a most amusing broadcast from the liner's nursery wing.

We began the first broadcast at 2.00 in the after-

A World in Your Ear

noon, with listeners hearing from the microphone on the dockside at Southampton all the bustle of boarding, and from others on board the sounds of the liner as she prepared to sail. At 3.30 the microphone on board relayed the hauling in of the anchor and the throbbing of the great engines, and at 3.45 those on the dock picked up the noisy goodbye scenes as the ship sailed away. We also planned to broadcast a 45-minute tour of the ship on the second night out, as well as some concerts and the like.

But the whole conception had captured the imagination of far more than just the British public. By the time we sailed, radio men from America, France, Germany and Holland had joined us, and I was asked to arrange live broadcasts for them all, on whatever waveband they needed. I was planning on two daily newsflashes for the BBC and an occasional direct broadcast for each respective foreign team. But soon a sort of fever set in, and in the four-day trip we finally made 56 live broadcasts, to Britain and the empire, Europe and America, and I don't think I saw the bed in my sumptuous cabin once. The two American commentators, Fred Bate of NBC and Frank Royal, were marvellous company, but most persuasive arm-twisters when it came to asking for extra broadcasts.

One guest aboard the liner was the general marine manager of the Radio Communication Company, the firm that had designed and supplied the original installation used by 2ZY Manchester, and it was interesting to talk to him about those early days. One

Baldwin and the Boat Race

of his staff pestered me for an introduction to the BBC, and this I performed for him. I was to do the same a year later in Paris for a young man who became a renowned BBC figure. Why did they approach me? I was told I was too accommodating: everyone else gave these young hopefuls the brush-off. But I believed in helping anyone who showed real keenness.

By the time we docked at Pier 90, New York Harbour, I was exhausted. It was midday and the temperature was soaring; I longed for a shower and bed. Fred Bate kindly sought me out and explained that he had a car standing by and he would escort me to my hotel, the St Regis on Fifth Avenue. By this time I was past caring, and sank into the immense limousine grateful that someone else was making the arrangements. But it was not to be as simple as that, because Fred then informed me that in a few seconds I would be on the air: he had arranged to interview me for all the American networks from the radio-equipped car.

It was my first taste of American know-how and nerve, and I was hugely impressed. After the broadcast, still in a state of shock and with my mind fully on that shower, I listened vaguely to him briefing me about American traditions. He was still yelling while I got to my room, practically sleep-walking, and fumbled with the taps of the shower. Patiently Fred pointed to the hot tap. I reached out and turned it, and icy water cascaded over me. I yelled and leapt out, while he roared with laughter, and a tumbler was pushed into my trembling hand. It was pure rye whisky. I became wide awake with shock — and remained awake for the rest of my stay in America.

Fred, who was chief of programmes and senior commentator with NBC, Edward Cohen (CBS senior executive engineer), Mr C. Saerchinger (a famous high-speed CBS commentator) and Mr O.B. Hanson (NBC chief engineer) made sure my stay in America was memorable. They took me to one of their transmitting stations in the country, gave me the run of Radio City, and asked me to speak at a number of important gatherings.

One of the things they showed me that really caught my eye was NBC's prototype of a centimetre-wavelength transmitter, which I saw in production. This was so tiny it could be housed comfortably in a top hat or shoulder bag for race meetings, 'sidewalk' interviews and so on. When I got back to England I set to work at once to try and make one for myself. It was later developed by our research department for use over short distances and for unobtrusive interviews. It eliminated the need for a connecting cable, and gave us the flexibility to go where we wanted with no trailing leads. Thus it was a forerunner of the modern miniature portable radio microphone, and a most valuable souvenir of my trip. I proved its usefulness to the BBC's chief engineer by sending it down the great Wookey Hole pot-hole, and although it met with unavoidable interference from mineral elements in the earth, it worked. Then I took it down to Sandwich and asked a former professional golfer

Baldwin and the Boat Race

who was now a commentator to try it out strapped to his back. Equipped with it he was able to follow the golfers around the course. He could only go a short distance that first time, but it proved my point.

My most vivid memory of New York was the wonderful turn-out of the New York Fire Brigade. I happened to mention one evening to Fred and my other friends that I had often seen them in action on films, and thought it must be marvellous to see them in real life. A few minutes later I went into my bedroom to change as we were having a little farewell party, and no sooner had I opened the door than there came to my ears the most powerful clanging of bells and sirens I had ever heard in my life. I shot over to the window and there were several fire engines, speeding past my hotel. And down on the street too, with both hands clasped over his head like a boxer acknowledging the applause, was Fred Bate, taking personal credit for the whole performance. When I got downstairs everyone was grinning all over their faces. It had been pure chance, but they were delighted I had been able to see the real thing. The Americans I met on that trip were a splendid bunch of people, helpful, friendly and amusing, and I've never forgotten them.

Eventually I made my way back to the harbour for the homeward voyage. On returning to my cabin I found gifts and letters from the friends I had made in America, and remembered their many tempting offers to me. But I had been shaken by the tempo of life and work in New York, and was glad to take things

A World in Your Ear

quietly on the journey home.

Having seen one magnificent fire brigade at work, I was very soon to be involved with another. I had just arrived home from work one autumn evening in 1936 and was settling down to a meal when the telephone rang and I heard the director of outside broadcasting saying to me, 'If you look out of your window, you'll see a flame on the horizon.' I dropped the receiver and rushed to the window and indeed there was a flame, for the Crystal Palace was on fire.

He asked if there was any chance of my getting across to the fire right away and possibly doing a broadcast from the scene. I automatically said yes — I don't think I have ever refused an outside broadcast in my life — and I immediately tried to telephone any engineer who might still be at the BBC, though it was getting late. Luckily I found Mr Crouch, a senior assistant, who at once promised to try and get a set of equipment down by van. I arranged to meet him somewhere along the Parade in front of the burning Palace, and set off in my old Vauxhall which, according to my usual practice, had a spare set of basic outside broadcasting equipment in the boot.

By the time I reached Streatham Common I found hundreds of others had had the same idea and the road was blocked with vehicles all the way to the Palace. But fire engines were converging from all quarters, and as one group tore past I just fell in behind them and achieved a non-stop passage to the Parade. It was strewn with firemen and their equipment: the heat was terrific and molten glass was

Baldwin and the Boat Race

flying and smashing everywhere. I pulled up, and almost at once ran into my good friend Commander Firebrace.

'What on earth are you doing here?' he demanded. I explained that I hoped to do a live broadcast from the scene, and he tartly wished me luck and pressed on with his job. First I needed a telephone line, but in those days public call boxes were few and far between. I looked around for wires and discovered that a small café on a corner of the Parade had a telephone. I ran over and asked the owner if I could use it; he looked at me bemused. He obviously felt his whole business was crumbling around him — for, with the loss of the Palace, all his trade was likely to vanish — but I explained how urgent it was and pressed a few notes into his trembling hand, and he agreed.

I got through to the GPO operator and asked if I could be connected on an uninterrupted line to the control room at Broadcasting House. I had some cheek really, but they agreed. At this point the intrepid Mr Crouch arrived with the outside broadcasting van and we started to rig up a microphone.

Then we went on to the roof of the café, searching among the crowd for our commentator. The fire had been reported on the 9.00 news, and this sent thousands more spectators hurrying to watch the blaze, so our search might have seemed hopeless. But our commentator that night was the head of outside broadcasting himself and he had one outstanding feature. He stood six foot eight inches tall, a fair-haired giant said to be the only man who could look down on Sir John Reith, and even in such a crowd you could easily spot him. Soon he joined us on the roof of the café, and we gave the go-ahead to the control room.

Our commandeered GPO line worked perfectly, and after a brief announcement our live commentary from the fire was on the air — crackling flames, splintering glass and all. The following evening I was asked to make a broadcast on the Home Service about the whole adventure: it was the first 'flying squad' outside broadcast.

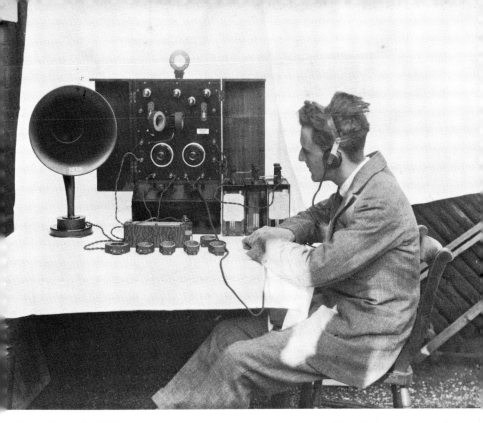

Robert Wood in 1921 with a radio receiver he designed and made himself.

Captain Peter Eckersley, the BBC's chief engineer in the early days. (*BBC copyright*)

3. J. C. W. Reith on the *Queen Mary*.

4. Robert Wood (left, in light suit) supervises the installation of the 'sausage-hoop' aerial on the roof of 2ZY, the BBC's Manchester station, on 28 January 1924.

5. Dan Godfrey, the first director of 2ZY, conducting in the station's studio. (*BBC copyright*)

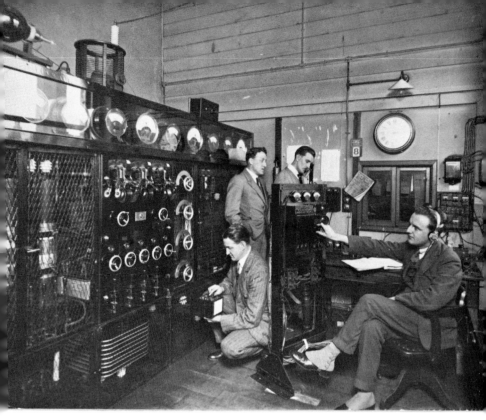

3. Robert Wood (right) at the controls of 2ZY's transmitter. Behind him is the window into the studio.

Wood on the terrace of the House of Commons controlling a live broadcast of Sir Alan Cobham's arrival by seaplane from Australia on October 1926.

8. Neville Chamberlain, arriving at Heston Airport from Munich in September 1938, reads the declaration of peace which he and Hitler had signed. (*Popperfoto*)

9. Winston Churchill broadcasts to the nation in spring 1940. (*Radio Times Hulton Picture Library*)

). The Crystal Palace is destroyed by fire on 1 December 1936. (*Radio Times Hulton Picture brary*)

. King George VI broadcasts on Christmas Day 1944. (*BBC copyright*)

12. Princess Elizabeth (right) and Princess Margaret. (*Keystone*)

13. *Old Mother Red Riding Boots*, the Christmas pantomime at Windsor Castle in 1944. (*Radio Times Hulton Picture Library*)

14. Richard Dimbleby in the commentator's box in the triforium of Westminster Abbey during rehearsal for the 1953 coronation. (*Popperfoto*)

15. The state procession down the nave after the ceremony. (*Keystone*)

16. Howard Marshall. (*BBC copyright*)

17. John Snagge. (*Popperfoto*)

4

'Look after the king'

Events more serious than the Crystal Palace fire were looming, however, throughout that autumn of 1936. The Prince of Wales, who had played such a noteworthy part as the glamorous heir to the throne, much in evidence at functions, garden parties and nightclubs, and loved by everyone, was now king. But the world resounded with rumours about him and Mrs Simpson. People abroad probably knew more than we did, for his Mediterranean trips with her were written up in the foreign press and not in our own.

The first I knew of what was really developing was early in December when Sir John Reith asked me in strict confidence unobtrusively to install equipment and organize GPO circuits at Windsor Castle, because a possible broadcast to the nation was 'in the air'.

It was one of those busy periods in my life when I could have been doing two or three other things all the time; everything piled up. But that evening, after work so that no-one would ask questions, I went down to Windsor. I was already well known there, and with the help of the Master of the Household I installed my equipment, finishing around midnight. The study we would use for the broadcast overlooked

A World in Your Ear

the quadrangle and my equipment was outside in the corridor.

The following evening I went there straight from the office and just waited. I had to be discreet, though the castle staff were kind enough to give me a meal. Meals, however, were never a priority in the outside broadcaster's life; we often had to skip them. My job was simply to be ready, for when parliament was informed of the king's decision, one of the first men to be told of it would be Sir John Reith. He would then drive down to Windsor and expect to find me there. For four days running I travelled down to Windsor after work without telling anyone, and waited; but nothing happened. On the final evening I stood out for a while on the Round Tower. The castle looked very peaceful, with moonlight streaming down out of a clear and beautiful sky on to the great grounds and ancient walls, and the Thames running quietly past, and I thought to myself, 'I can't understand you, giving up all this.'

Eventually, on 11 December, Sir John arrived and we both waited. Then the king came in. He had been with his family the whole afternoon, particularly with his mother, having discussions. But this was the end. He simply sat down and made his broadcast. I don't think Reith could grasp it, and I was just amazed. We couldn't appreciate the fact that it was all over. Nowadays people grow up knowing a king has abdicated, but to us then it seemed unbelievable. King Edward, however, looked quite natural throughout, not at all at the end of his tether. He was always

'Look after the king'

a good broadcaster, especially when he'd had a little to drink, which was sometimes the case. He delivered his speech quite simply, and I found myself rather moved, even though I was there with him — more moved than *he* was, I would say. Then he said goodbye and the next thing we heard was the Daimler whizzing out of the gates, to the coast and then to France. I returned home wondering what could happen next.

That broadcast was soon followed by the proclamation of the new king, George VI, and Queen Elizabeth, from the same balcony at St James's Palace that Edward VIII had been proclaimed from only a few months earlier. My arrangements for the live coverage of the event followed the same pattern.

Soon after this came the most momentous event of my career. I was sitting at my desk one morning when a call came that Sir John Reith wanted me. I reported to him at once and he simply told me: 'We are going on a journey.' We went down to his car and set off. I tried to think where we were heading, but my calculations were thrown out when he leaned forward and asked me if I'd like a cigarette. Now Reith did not smoke, nor did he encourage his employees to smoke in the early days of the BBC: it was a brave man who lit a cigarette in the office. So where on earth could we be going, I wondered, that he felt my nerves might need steadying with tobacco?

Suddenly the car drew up. We had stopped in front of Buckingham Palace. Sir John opened the car door and waved at me to get out. 'Go in, they're expecting you,' he said. And added: 'The king has got a lot of

A World in Your Ear

broadcasting to do. Make a good broadcaster of him.'

It was 11.00 in the morning. I got out in a daze, and walked through the gate and straight in. An equerry was waiting and I was taken upstairs to meet the king. I had met him briefly already, when he had carried out broadcasts at various functions as the Duke of York, but I had not met him as king.

I was escorted into the audience room and found myself face to face with King George VI and Queen Elizabeth. Queen Elizabeth began the conversation and made things very easy for me. They knew what I was there for, because Reith had arranged it all without telling me. The problem behind my visit was that the king had a lot of responses to make in the forthcoming coronation service, and would also have to make a speech to the nation the same evening. It was widely known that he suffered from a very heavy stammer, and it was now my job to help him minimize the effects of this in his broadcast.

I began by doing rehearsals with the king as he had always done them, standing up at a sort of high ledger desk. This was the way he had been coached by his speech therapist, who believed that standing helped him to speak more clearly, and the king thought it was necessary. But it seemed most uncomfortable and, little by little over the years, I managed to get him down till he was able to sit at ease at a desk like every other broadcaster. It was very difficult for me. I had to be very tactful because I was not a famous Harley Street specialist; I was only a specialist in microphones, and it took time to overcome this and

'Look after the king'

win his trust. But we did it. It was hard for the king too, because you could see how he had suffered all his life because of his impediment and you could not help but feel sorry for him. Little by little I helped him with tone formation and lip formation, and showed him how he could let the microphone do the work.

I also tried to find a way round obvious difficulties, pointing out words in the script that might trip him up. We would discuss them and he usually accepted my suggestions. Sometimes he would disagree and argue that the word in question was one he could pronounce with no difficulty. I remember that during the war he used to have great difficulty saying 'oppression' and 'suppression', words that in those dark days came up all too often. The king protested that he could say them perfectly well, which he certainly could if he took his time and concentrated only on them. But it was a different matter in the middle of a speech. I wouldn't argue, but used to turn the conversation to other matters and then, out of the blue, challenge him: 'Say "oppression" and "suppression".' Caught unawares, he would try, trip up on those infernal Ss and then give up with good humour. It became a sort of training school, and the king struggled without let-up. I was full of admiration for his perseverence, his resolution. Over the years he learnt how to cope, and eventually became a master of the microphone.

Preparations were going ahead for the coverage of the coronation, the most complicated broadcast the

A World in Your Ear

BBC had ever attempted. I spent months in planning and discussions with the earl marshal's office, deciding coverage of the whole event from the moment the gilded coaches left Buckingham Palace right through to the end of the coronation service in Westminster Abbey. We were faced with continuous broadcasting from 10.00 in the morning till 5.30 at night, and I would not be able to leave my control room during all that time.

The whole system of wiring, both inside the abbey and along the processional route, was carried out by GPO engineers under my direction. We not only had to have lines connecting each microphone to one of the two control rooms and to the respective control rooms of Broadcasting House and the International Trunk Exchange, but two-way communication had also to be maintained between all these points. And every circuit had to be duplicated as far as possible, in case of breakdown. In the end we used 472 miles of wire and 12 tons of equipment. 60 BBC engineers were engaged on the broadcast, and I had to think of all sorts of details, even down to the hiring of full morning dress for the engineers working inside the abbey — complete with top hats and grey gloves.

Our two control rooms were at Westminster Abbey (for the home and empire programmes) and at the Middlesex Guildhall (for all the foreign commentators). In addition to two commentaries for the United States, the service was also covered in Czech, Danish, Dutch, Finnish, Flemish, French, German, Hungarian, Japanese, Norwegian, Spanish (for South America),

'Look after the king'

Swedish and Serbo-Croat. The French commentator was the distinguished writer André Maurois. The English commentary began with John Snagge, and Howard Marshall picked it up from within the abbey.

I set up 58 microphones. 11 were strung along the route to accommodate the BBC commentators and catch the crowd noises and the music; I had effects microphones strung up over the gate at Buckingham Palace through which the state coach would pass, down the Mall, along Whitehall past the Cenotaph, in Parliament Square and over the great door of the abbey. A further 15 were provided for the overseas commentators and I had placed 32 within the abbey itself. Again we did a nice little job of camouflage, hiding them in chinks of masonry, under prayer stools, in chandeliers and lecterns. We even managed to tuck one into each arm of Edward the Confessor's chair, which would be used for the actual enthronement, and put a third on its carved back. The results more than rewarded us. I don't think anyone who heard the music of the service, and the voices of the choirboys soaring higher and higher, will ever forget it.

All 58 microphones terminated on the panel of my room in the abbey. Here I could control the volume and amplify the signal before it was fed to the transmitters at Broadcasting House. But it was also fed to the foreign control room, to provide a background of effects for the overseas commentators, and to the loudspeakers placed along the processional route, so that the crowds could listen to the service from the abbey. Outputs were also provided to carry

A World in Your Ear

my sound for recording as a soundtrack for the various newsreel films that were being made of the event.

The programme was also fed back to each observation point so that the BBC commentators could pick up the description from one another easily. An elaborate series of cue sentences was devised, so that each commentator could indicate to the next one along the route that his description was finished, and he could pick up smoothly, without a break. There was no clumsy 'Over to you now, Nigel' in that broadcast.

I had to memorize, weeks in advance, every last detail of the seven-and-a-half-hour broadcast, from the palace to the crowning, for with no closed-circuit television monitor it was, once more, the old story of precision timing and memory that guided me as to when to fade out one microphone and fade in the next. But where I had used 12 microphones for the Duke of Kent's wedding, now I had 32 within the abbey, and an infinitely more complicated ceremony. For in 1937 two monarchs were crowned, King George VI and Queen Elizabeth, in two separate ceremonies. This meant the service was far longer than the single coronation of Queen Elizabeth II, which I also covered in 1953 — with a television screen at my side.

With so many microphones, the combination faded in at any one time has to be very carefully watched so that the sound is not jumbled or the circuits overloaded. For instance, during that part of the service

'Look after the king'

called 'The Recognition' when the archbishop presents the monarch to north, south, east and west, they both moved some considerable distance from the nearest possible microphone, and after the quiet voice of the archbishop, the shouted response of the peers and peeresses and the fanfare that followed would reverberate through everything if I did not watch it carefully. I was in a state of constant tension as I sat in the control room, trying through all the long hours to convey to the listener the greatness and the majesty of the occasion.

It was an event for which I should have prepared, I suspect, like an athlete, building up my stamina as if for a marathon run and getting lots of sleep. Unfortunately my superiors had an irrational but probably understandable fear that I would break a leg or get run over by a bus on my way to the abbey, and that would have ruined everything. So they hit on the brilliant idea of having me spend the night not just in town, but safely installed in the abbey itself. They fitted out a tiny store-room next door to the control room, and I was left there, locked in the abbey along with some of the most valuable church plate in the world, which was on display for this all-important occasion and glowing in the dim light of the stained-glass windows.

What my anxious superiors had forgotten completely was that the abbey is just across the road from parliament and dear old Big Ben. All through the night, every 15 minutes, I was shattered by the crashing sound of the great clock chiming the quarters

A World in Your Ear

and the hours. I knew the sound well, for it was I who had wired Big Ben up for broadcasting some time before. But if anyone thought it was possible to sleep through that din, they were sadly mistaken. In the end I gave up the idea, smoked far too many cigarettes and began reading and re-reading the service. I took a few walks round the abbey, but would have liked to have been able to open the doors and get a breath of fresh air.

In the event, I did not break a leg and nor did anyone else. The service went off marvellously. King George VI was crowned and dedicated and then Queen Elizabeth was crowned in her own separate and most moving ceremony. During the homeward journey of the procession we used a different approach from that on the outward journey. No commentary was heard; instead four special 'atmosphere' microphones told the whole story by picking up the effects and the responses of the people in the crowd as the pageant passed along the Embankment, across Trafalgar Square, through the Mall, past St James's Palace to Piccadilly Circus and on to Constitution Hill.

Coronation fever had reached an extraordinary pitch by the time the date, 12 May, arrived. Perhaps in order to put the debacle of the last king's brief reign behind them, people were trying to stamp this as the 'real' coronation. Streets and buildings in London were decorated with red, white, blue and royal purple. The great stores competed with each other to obtain the most striking effect, with flags,

'Look after the king'

banners, trappings of all kinds and façades decorated with life-size pictures of the kings and queens of history, and at night there was tremendous splendour, with floodlighting and fairy lights on a scale never attempted before.

Almost the only element missing were London's famous red double-decker buses, for their drivers had chosen this moment to strike. Perhaps it was just as well. With so many visitors thronging the streets, the usual load of buses as well might easily have brought the capital to a standstill.

I had anticipated the crowds and the difficulties they might cause, for after the coronation was over I had to hurry to Buckingham Palace where the king was to broadcast to the world that evening. Realizing a few days before the event that half of London would be heading for the palace at the same time, I asked Sir Alexander Hardinge, the king's private secretary, for some sort of permit that would get me through the police barriers on foot as fast as possible: there was no hope of getting a car near Buckingham Palace. This he arranged and it worked wonders, though I had to have a policeman's help to fight through the crowds outside the abbey as I left, and another burly policeman to help me through the huge throng outside the palace when I got there. It was coronation night and everyone seemed determined to spend it outside the palace gates.

I set to work there testing my equipment. We were using two ordinary BBC microphones (one the usual spare). The BBC had prepared two microphones and a matching signal light mounted in cases of Australian oak, 14 inches high, to be used in royal broadcasts. But King George VI disliked them, saying the design reminded him of the Cenotaph, so although they were always set up for appearances' sake when photographs were being taken of a royal broadcast, what we actually used were the small, standard moving coil microphones. Churchill was later offered the ornate monsters and rejected them on the same grounds.

Sir John Reith, who had been a guest at the abbey ceremony, arrived before the king's broadcast just in time to save me from losing my temper completely. The programme producer at Broadcasting House was in a flap that evening and wanted an early speech test from the king, which I felt was unnecessary. The king, after all, had just spent the most demanding, emotional and exhausting day of his life, and voice rehearsals were the last thing he needed. For my own part, I felt that if I had managed to control the immense complexity of the coronation broadcast without a hitch, I could certainly handle this with no further rehearsal. Consequently the telephone kept ringing in my control room as my critics at Broadcasting House demanded that a final rehearsal by the king should be passed to them for approval. I flatly refused. Sir John realized that I was having some difficulty in controlling my temper and said a few sharp words into the telephone. Peace reigned at last.

Just after the broadcast, which despite the fears of the BBC producer went off perfectly, the king

'Look after the king'

beckoned me forward and pinned the coronation medal on me 'as a memento of the occasion'. Then he and the queen had to return to the balcony to wave to the crowds who did not want to let them go. 'We want the king,' came the incessant roar from below. 'What the king would like most is his dinner,' confessed the monarch in a whispered aside. In a typically thoughtful gesture, he had dismissed most of his staff so that they, too, could join the celebrations.

By this time I was completely drained of energy and very tired. I wanted to get home to my family and relax and start to prepare for a long list of coronation-year outside broadcasts which lay ahead of me, including a naval and an army review. A day or two earlier I had left my car at Broadcasting House. I was planning to go and pick it up when a message came through from my chief, telephoning from the control room there, inviting me to join them at a celebration dinner at Paganis, then a well-known restaurant in Great Portland Street. There were many traffic diversions because of the crowds celebrating in the West End, so I had a long and tedious journey from the palace to Broadcasting House to collect my car, and I was even more exhausted by the time I arrived at the celebration dinner around 11 p.m. I found myself unable to eat much, or take in much. I just had a couple of large brandies, and around midnight I excused myself and set off for home. I arrived home about 1.30 and at last fell into those welcoming sheets. The great day was over — at last.

A World in Your Ear

I was not left to rest on my laurels for long, for the keynote of outside broadcasting is unpredictability, and you learn to watch for the unlikely and even expect it to happen. This was brought home to me vividly just a week after the coronation when the great coronation naval review of 1937 took place and we hit an unsuspected rock.

All 'friendly' nations were taking part in the review, which was to be a greater spectacle than even the jubilee review of George V, and we found our previous experience invaluable. This time the 'coffin' transmitter, together with two commentators and me, were housed on board *HMS Nelson*. Radio signals were again relayed to Southsea Castle, my friends on *HMS Collingwood*, the Royal Navy communication headquarters at Portsmouth, were lending assistance wherever necessary, and it looked as though everything would be ship-shape and trouble-free.

The principal commentator was the likeable Lieutenant-Commander Tommy Woodrooffe, who already that year had covered the Derby, the Grand National, and the coronation with a magnificent description of the scene from the top of Constitution Hill. He was, of course, now retired from the Royal Navy, but obviously particularly well qualified to describe what was taking place. Unfortunately, he was sent to 'pick up some atmosphere' on *HMS Nelson*, the ship on which he had begun his own training as a rookie, and his many friends took the opportunity of renewing their acquaintance. The reunion became something of a prolonged celebration and when he

'Look after the king'

eventually arrived for the broadcast both the captain and I were rather concerned about his over-confident manner.

I signalled a message to Broadcasting House warning them of the position, but at that moment, since the commentary had to begin, there was nothing we could do but fade him in. His narration was jocular, and became increasingly carefree minute by minute. An amusing atmosphere was generated as the nation listened, and presumably more and more people turned to their neighbours and said something like, 'Hey, listen to this, I think this bloke on the BBC's a bit merry.' Anyone who had the fortune to hear the broadcast will remember a few of Tommy's expressions which appeared to be repeated with remarkable frequency such as 'The fleet's lit up' — nothing unusual in that, it was taking place at night; but 'The sky's below' did require a little more explanation, and several other phrases seemed to indicate that his judgment was about 180 degrees out of true. It was like reliving my old days as an emergency newsreader in Manchester — only this time there was no lift rope to grab.

I sat helpless, not knowing what to do about this unusual commentary which was booming out everywhere. I tried cutting into his monitoring headphones in the hope that I could gently cue him out, but he ignored me and went on talking. In the end I simply faded him out, still talking, and raced up to the commentary position where we exchanged several impolite words. The captain and his aides contacted

A World in Your Ear

me immediately and all I could do was apologize to them. The fleet took to sea for manoeuvres, and I despondently returned to my cabin.

A little while later I was woken up by a knock at my cabin door. A rating told me that the duty officer wished to see me immediately. It turned out that Tommy had escaped from the cabin into which he had been discreetly locked, and was thoroughly enjoying himself in the officers' mess, which he had opened up. I went down and managed by persuasion and intimidation to get him back safely into bed.

Next morning the fleet returned to port and Tommy and I travelled back to London. We were summoned to a full inquest, conducted by the late Sir Basil E. Nicholls, who was then head of programmes. I was very disappointed by the broadcast, considering the time and work put in by everyone concerned. And I heard later that there had been unfavourable repercussions aboard *HMS Nelson*, which was a pity because everyone from the captain down had put themselves out to ensure that any facilities we might require were available. But some people saw the funny side. My old friend George Black, director of the variety theatre chain, quickly staged a new revue entitled *The Fleet's Lit Up* and it ran very successfully.

At Christmas that year the new king resumed the habit begun by his father George V of giving a Christmas Day speech to the nation and the empire. These had begun in 1932 at Sandringham and I took over sole responsibility for them at Reith's direction in 1935. Although Edward VIII had not been on the

'Look after the king'

throne long enough to continue the tradition (he acceded in January and abdicated in early December), George VI was anxious to do so. The king always wrote his own speech for the Christmas Day broadcast, with the help of Queen Elizabeth, for they worked together as a team. If they didn't like the sound of a passage during rehearsal they would go away together and work on it, crossing things out, trying new phrases until they had exactly what they wanted, and what they meant — and what the king could say without difficulty. There were no glib speechwriters for him. He and Queen Elizabeth were unfailingly hard-working, dedicated and considerate, and I felt privileged to serve them.

The Christmas broadcasts were always live. There was a phrase in one of the first ones that the king often referred to later, about how 'the sailor on the sea and the shepherd on the hills' were joining together with all the rest of the other listeners for this Christmas message. King George VI would often remark that 'If the shepherd on the hills is willing to listen to me, I am willing to speak to him'. The disruption of his Christmas Day with the family was accepted as one more duty that came with the job.

It meant Christmas away from the family for me. I always had to travel down the night before, for Sandringham is a very isolated place in Norfolk which I could not guarantee to reach safely on Christmas Day from Merton. So I would go down through King's Lynn the day before and stay in Sandringham village after installing and checking my equipment.

A World in Your Ear

We would rehearse with the king sometimes on Christmas Eve, sometimes on Christmas Day morning, invariably after his return from church; we would have another rehearsal about 2.15 and then the broadcast itself promptly at 3.00. There was no producer there apart from me.

I used to take four hundredweight of equipment with me, which was installed in a small room next to the king's study. On Christmas Eve I would make test runs on the lines to Broadcasting House to check that everything was working properly. As always for important broadcasts, I set up two microphones, one as a spare. At a few minutes to 3.00 the king would leave the other members of the family and go to his study where, seated in his chair, he watched for the flashing red light on his desk that gave him the signal to begin. In those days the message was the focal point of the day for most people living in Britain or the Commonwealth, and it was estimated that the king had an audience of at least 400 million.

It was always something of an ordeal for the king, though he very much wanted to do it. I remember an incident one Christmas Day when a younger member of the royal family was trying unsuccessfully to catch his interest in some event and the king suddenly burst out, 'I can't concentrate on anything because I've got that damned broadcast coming up this afternoon.' He felt he could not relax and start to enjoy the family Christmas until it was successfully completed. I shared his feelings. For in my family the Christmas turkey was always eaten on Boxing Day — after we'd

'Look after the king'

dismantled the equipment and driven home with it on Christmas Day evening. And one of the benefits of the war — for like all clouds that, too, had some flashes of silver lining — was the fact that throughout it the royal family stayed in Windsor, which meant I could get there and back in one day.

Despite the great events I was now involved in, from 1935 onwards radio was no longer my only concern. On 2 November 1936 the world's first television centre at Alexandra Palace started transmitting. At the head of this magic lantern were Gerald Cock, the BBC's first director of television, and Leonard Schuster. Both of them had moved there from their respective positions as programme head and executive head of outside broadcasts on the sound side, and perhaps it was because of this that Gerald Cock insisted from the outset that I should be given responsibility for all televised outside broadcasts. This was agreed, though I never asked for it, nor indeed wanted it. Nor was I ever paid a penny more for doing two jobs instead of one, though I already had enough on my plate in radio.

Soon after my appointment we were given two fully equipped mobile cable-feed control vans as well as a transmitter with its own independent power supply in another van. This equipment had been built by the Marconi—EMI Television Company and made reception possible from practically any point within a 20-mile radius of the transmitting station.

My staff was increased, but only a few of them had

A World in Your Ear

any television know-how. There was no published information at all. Once again, as in the early days in Manchester, we had to start from scratch. First we had to find good cameramen, but they had to be electrically-minded. Filming with a newsreel camera is a different matter: the cameraman, with clockwork or battery, is simply recording the images he sees. But a television cameraman is scanning the article with an electronic camera, making certain corrections as he does so, and the output of that camera is fed to many different units to make up the different components of the picture. It is a lot more complicated than taking a roll of simple film which you can send off anywhere for processing.

We set off at once, in November 1936, covering all sorts of events for television, including golf, riding and boxing; we televised part of the coronation too. Cameras were not permitted in the abbey, but three were installed at Apsley Gate at Hyde Park Corner, and an eight-mile cable was laid by the GPO from there to Alexandra Palace. The BBC's four-ton TV van made its first appearance here, and despite the bad weather over 10,000 viewers picked up the transmission, within a radius of some 60 miles, on screens that measured ten inches by eight inches. We went on to cover tennis from Wimbledon, the Lord Mayor's Show, the Cenotaph ceremony on Armistice Day, my old friend the pets' corner at London Zoo, and film-making in progress at Pinewood, Denham and Elstree.

But the preparations for television coverage always

'*Look after the king*'

took far longer than for a sound broadcast and it was therefore considerably more expensive than radio. There were also physical limitations which we always had to consider. We could only take cables so far. We had to have a power van, a large vehicle that supplied power for the scanning van, which was also the control room. These mobile camera control rooms had facilities for feeding video-frequencies into special GPO cables which ran underground at strategic points and terminated in the vision control room at Alexandra Palace. These frequencies were then radiated for the public to receive in picture form on a television screen.

This use of cable imposed restrictions, however, in the form of distortion, attenuation, electrical interference and, in the long run, the limited lengths of cable available. To enable us to travel further afield and cover even more important events, Marconi—EMI produced a mobile video-transmitter with its own generators. But care had to be exercised in siting the generator van so that its own noise would not be picked up on the microphone. You also needed a site where you could transmit a good signal. The siting of these vans was a big headache. Not only were they temperamental, they were also huge — about two-thirds the size of a London bus — and not the sort of thing you could place casually next to Wimbledon centre court without ruining things for the spectators.

The man at my right hand at this time was Mr T.H.Bridgewater, who had worked as an engineer with the Baird Television Company and was one of

A World in Your Ear

the few people who really knew a lot about television. He eventually became chief engineer of our TV centre. Marconi—EMI also assigned an experienced engineer to each of the two mobile units to give on-the-spot training and advice to my staff, and Mr Bridgewater did all he could through lectures and talks to help prepare them for their job. For we were once again handling equipment without any adequate experience. In what little spare time I had, I collected all the information I could and amplified it into written matter for the use of my staff. Otherwise very few senior engineers in the corporation knew anything about television. The BBC rushed to get started and be first in the field, with everyone pressing me to the limit. But while the early radio experiments had been fairly cheap to run and simple to arrange, television was costly and complicated. So once more we found ourselves the babies, the beginners, but this time out in the open air, not in a nice little studio.

In the summer of 1938 I went to Paris to cover for radio the unveiling by King George VI of a World War I memorial in the military cemetery at Viller, Bretonneux. Since my first meeting with the king, I had handled all his broadcasts, though it sometimes caused me problems. After I had reported back to Sir John Reith on that first meeting, he had instructed me: 'Don't tell anyone where you're going. Just attend whenever they want you, no matter what else you have on hand, and look after the king personally.'

This was to lead to some difficult situations for me. A rehearsal of each speech would take place in

'Look after the king'

private at Buckingham Palace and that meant disappearing for some time. I had to work to verbal appointments made directly by the king's successive private secretaries, and I got to know a succession of these dedicated men — Sir Eric Miéville, Sir Alexander Hardinge, Sir Alan Lascelles, Sir Piers Leigh, Sir Michael Adeane and Sir Edward Ford.

This put me in a most unenviable situation with my superiors, who resented my sudden and inexplicable disappearances and felt they had a right to know where I was. But when I spoke of this to Sir John he simply retorted: 'You work to me on such matters,' and that was that. He felt the king's business must be completely confidential.

So on 22 July 1938 I was in France, and the commentators and I were enjoying a few day's stay at a hotel next to the Champs Elysées. It was my first stay in Paris and I was looking for someone to show me a little of the city, when a young Englishman approached us in the hotel and introduced himself. He appeared to have time on his hands and explained that he was rather hard up and without a job. But he knew Paris like the back of his hand, since his parents were based in the capital. As he was free, I said: 'I'll tell you what I'll do. I'd like to see something of Paris while I'm here. I'll pay for the taxi and the meal if you'll take me on a tour.' So we hired a taxi (they were not expensive in those days) and that's what we did.

I discovered he could talk well and most interestingly. We went on a little shopping expedition to buy

A World in Your Ear

presents for my family, and he asked my advice on what would be a suitable present for a toddler: one of his sons was having a birthday and he wanted to buy him something, hard up though he was. I told him the sort of toys my son Bill enjoyed and altogether we got on very well.

Anyway, he made quite an impression on me, and I liked to help when I could — perhaps it was the old trade unionist in me. My friend had said his one ambition was to join the BBC, so when I got back to London I made a point of talking to Lindsay Wellington, a senior programme official who was a great confidant of mine. I told him that I had met a young man in Paris called Richard Dimbleby, who had impressed me with his knowledge and ability to talk, and Wellington said he would do something. Soon after this Dimbleby got one or two appointments at the BBC and at once proved his worth. Richard and I were to work together on many assignments after that, especially the great ceremonial occasions which he made his own. In fact they became so associated with him that after the war, when he was at the height of his fame, a member of the royal family's staff whispered to me at a state function, 'Soon we'll have to ask Dimbleby's permission before we hold a coronation!'

Lindsay Wellington, later Sir Lindsay Wellington, who gave Dimbleby his first chance, was a man of outstanding integrity, the only man in my opinion who had all the attributes needed to succeed Sir John Reith. We lost a great man that year when Sir John

'Look after the king'

was persuaded to resign to take over Imperial Airways. It was just a silly manoeuvre by his enemies, who were hoping to take over the BBC with a war coming. Reith was a man apart. He set the foundations of the BBC — and they were reinforced-concrete foundations. To my mind Lindsay Wellington was the only man who could have replaced him. He had a sure broadcasting instinct and was the only one I felt I could rely on. But he was passed over, and the BBC suffered.

At that point in 1938, however, a more practical problem was facing me. The equipment we had been using for outside broadcasts was sadly out of date, and new equipment was being specially developed to replace it. We had not been consulted on the design and lived in hope that the research department understood our needs. Finally, after waiting for several years, we were told we were to take delivery of a considerable number of sets of specially designed self-contained, foolproof outside broadcast equipment, called the OB7.

But when it arrived we received a great shock; each set of equipment occupied as much space as our elderly, cumbersome Boat-Race transmitter and was quite unsuitable for everyday practical use. This I thought was an appalling waste of many thousands of pounds of our cash allocation, apart from the months of design time. The research department should have had the sense to discuss the whole project with us, the people who had to handle, install and operate the equipment. Instead the bulk of it went straight into the outside broadcasting store at Chapel Mews, next to Broadcasting House, while other sets went to emergency control rooms. Many senior engineers at the BBC, who had best remain anonymous, secretly cheered when Hitler set my stores ablaze two years later. A landmine exploded in the centre of Portland Place on 8 December 1940 and fires burned in Broadcasting House for seven hours. There was a period of tension when the OB7 equipment remained unfortunately untouched while all around it burned, but in the end many sets of the apparatus were engulfed as the flames spread. Once again we thankfully returned to our outdated and outmoded, but at least compact, equipment.

5

War of Words

In September 1938, the world was hanging in the balance. I found myself one day at Heston Airport, Heathrow, which in those days was simply a jumble of wooden huts with a control tower, waiting for the arrival of the prime minister, Neville Chamberlain, returning from his peace talks with Hitler at Munich. He came down from the aircraft and I positioned the microphone nearby so that he and his chief private secretary Lord Home could broadcast the verdict of the meeting for all the world. Everyone breathed a sigh of relief when they heard those historic words: 'From this nettle danger we have plucked the flower of peace.'

But not everyone was convinced. Certain senior people at the BBC decided it might be prudent to make certain preparations for what might turn out to be extremely important future broadcasts. I was asked to set about installing outside broadcasting equipment and duplicated GPO circuits on a semi-permanent basis to Broadcasting House from Windsor Castle, Buckingham Palace, 10 Downing Street, Chequers and the Central War Room. It was a gamble, but it more than paid off. In the years to come we

A World in Your Ear

were to use all these for a series of top-level maximum security broadcasts (see Appendix), though I sometimes blushed at the state of the outdated equipment I was forced to install. My vintage sets provoked sly comments in places like the Central War Room at Storey's Gate, where the various service technicians knew good from bad and were amused by what I had to make do with.

In the autumn of 1938 I was entertained to lunch by a man who was destined to become Sir Winston Churchill's aide and friend — General Lord Ismay, an outstanding wartime leader and a pillar of strength to everyone. We had a nice lunch and afterwards he said, 'Now Woody, you've been MI5'd. We know you're all right; and now the next person you're going to meet is Captain Babbiscombe.' Having MI5's approval meant I now had unrestricted access to confidential places, mainly that holy of holies the Central War Room, the underground headquarters of the cabinet and chiefs of staff. Lord Ismay was to dominate this nerve centre of operations and Captain Babbiscombe was the camp commandant. He was a severe man: nobody could get past him unless he knew them, and knew they had been approved. Lord Ismay hardly needed to check up on me. After all, I had been going to St James's Palace since 1925, I'd been to Buckingham Palace for the coronation and to Downing Street for every ministerial broadcast. I was well known.

I set about preparing for the worst. I supervised the installation by the GPO of the landlines. All were duplicated: one would be taken one way and the second by a different route altogether in case the first one was put out of action. You can't have all your eggs in one basket, nor all your cables double-banked in one circuit. I always laid two.

The various broadcasting points were numbered, Place One, Place Two and so on. During the war, when I was asked to go off to handle an important broadcast, the message was always 'Report to Place One' — it was unsafe to name the destination on the phone in case an enemy was listening — and then I would take myself off to Buckingham Palace or the Central War Room accordingly. It was fair to say that as 1939 arrived, I was better prepared than Neville Chamberlain.

By midsummer it was obvious that Hitler was still on the move and that Poland was going to be invaded. Flexible preparations were being made, air-raid precautions were being rehearsed and I was pressing ahead with my installations. On 1 September I was detailed to stay at the Clifton Hotel near Broadcasting House with a small number of my experienced assistants housed in the vicinity. Events were already crowding in. That day it was announced that television services were to be closed down for the duration. I was not sorry to lose the extra responsibilities of the infant TV service. Private and family life had just about ceased to exist for me and my staff and, with the war looming, these personal affairs were becoming increasingly precious and important.

It was a wonderful September and we pondered on the false cloud of security we had lived under since

A World in Your Ear

the Munich peace agreement 12 months before. Then came the announcement that the prime minister would make a statement to the nation at 11.00 on Sunday 3 September from Downing Street.

I went to Downing Street on the Saturday to make my arrangements, and spent the night there in the capable hands of the custodian and chief security officer, Mr Carter. I had known Mr Carter since the days of the BBC's first incursion there during the General Strike of 1926 and we were good friends. He knew everybody from kings and presidents to ambassadors, service chiefs and departmental heads, and he could sum up anyone who walked through the door. He was an emblem of security — severe, but frank and very likeable.

Sunday morning arrived. I took a walk over to the nearby War Room, checked the equipment there and saw that the circuits to Broadcasting House were in order. It was obvious that within a short space of time this would all become fully operational. I found Captain Babbiscombe already at his post with his assistant, a senior civil servant called George Rance. Also there that morning were many serious-faced service heads, and many armed security guards were well in evidence too.

I returned to Downing Street and found the Cabinet starting to arrive in strength. The prime minister did not look at all disturbed. I think that, probably alone of all those there, he still lived in a world of peace and goodwill, and still anticipated a reply from Hitler assuring him that all was well.

War of Words

The broadcast was scheduled for 11.00 and as the time drew near I did a speech test with Chamberlain. All the landlines were operational; I carried out a time check with Broadcasting House and warned the prime minister that he had only five minutes in hand. He proceeded to his seat in the Cabinet Room, now beginning to look worried. Everything was tense; the Cabinet waited outside in the vestibule looking very grave. It was absolutely silent in that great building. We were just waiting, because Chamberlain was waiting — for some message from somewhere to say that Hitler was going to reply. But Hitler said nothing. Minutes ticked by and the prime minister still hesitated. At Broadcasting House tension was high and I was on edge too. The Cabinet by this time were standing like wax figures and still Chamberlain sat, pale-faced and silent before the microphones. The time was 11.15 and finally I said to him, 'Sir, the world is waiting.'

He looked at me and replied, 'Well then, we'll make the announcement now.' And he proceeded to tell the world that a state of war now existed between Germany and Britain.

Personally I felt relieved in a curious way that at last we knew where we stood; a lot of other people felt the same sense of release. The atmosphere in Downing Street relaxed and became more like a scene on the Stock Exchange as everyone began to speculate on what would follow.

But speculation was short-lived, for almost immediately the air-raid sirens went off and everyone stood rigid. In fact it was simply a case of someone over-reacting to the enormity of the news they had just heard over the radio: the aircraft in question was a little British spotter plane flying over. But to my utter amazement the prime minister at once led the whole Cabinet down to his special air-raid shelter beneath the building. I could hardly believe my eyes. I went to the front door of Number 10, lit a cigarette and watched the people rushing about in confusion looking for shelters. It was a bright sunny morning and many people were on their way home from church. I looked around the deserted Cabinet Room and thought to myself, 'Well, if a little man with a moustache comes down now in a parachute he'll find a nice empty chair waiting for him in Downing Street!'

Soon the all-clear sounded as the mistake was realized, and before I'd finished my second cigarette the Cabinet had trooped rather sheepishly back and begun the business of waging all-out war. I reported to Mr Chamberlain that all our stations had transmitted his declaration. I had sensed during my telephone conversation with Broadcasting House that they were feeling a little shaky at the news; but Alvar Liddell, the senior duty announcer for the day, was a very stable man, and he, thank goodness, was unperturbed.

I then went off to Buckingham Palace to check the circuits to Broadcasting House and set up the microphones for the rehearsal and 6.00 p.m. broadcast by King George. I found everyone calm there, with an attitude of 'Well, this is it and we'll have to get on

War of Words

with it'. The king's broadcast went off smoothly and I set off to make my final visit to the Central War Room before returning to Broadcasting House. I found the BBC headquarters had already become a formidable and well-guarded stronghold, with passes and permits challenged at the door. Then at last I went back to the Clifton Hotel, which I had left two days earlier, for a good night's rest after a long and eventful day: Day One of the war.

One of my immediate difficulties was the disappearance of many of my finest staff, for they were snapped up by the services, particularly the Royal Air Force, where their knowledge of radio could be put to good use. I was left with a small, dedicated and usually overworked team of assistants who were often in considerable danger. They were a wonderful breed. World War II was, above all, the time when radio came into its own. With newspapers scarce, much reduced in size and censored, people turned to the BBC with the true sense that what they would hear would be accurate and informed. All over Europe forbidden sets helped to keep the people hopeful and encouraged in the face of German propaganda, while at home the radio was a lifeline of news, entertainment and shared emotion. It would have seemed a very long war indeed without those voices coming unfailingly over the air waves, and I marvelled at the stamina and courage of my staff, who spent long spells away from their families and loved ones.

In other departments of the BBC I felt that the changes brought about by the war were not always for the better. There, too, many of the best people had been called up, or indeed had volunteered for service. But it was not lost on some others that the BBC represented rather a safe job in a dangerous period. It was surprising how many well-placed and well-connected young gentlemen suddenly found themselves with unusual physical peculiarities which prevented them from performing active service, while equally suddenly finding themselves with a quite unsuspected taste for broadcasting. I looked back on that period as the Gold Rush, and wished that Reith were still director-general for he would never have allowed half of these untalented people to get in. But he had gone and the BBC grew bigger and less democratic.

I had little time to brood, however. In May 1940 after the tragedy of the fall of France and the British army's retreat through Dunkirk, Neville Chamberlain resigned and Winston Churchill took command. What a man! What a leader! What a microphone voice!

I had worked with Churchill before on outside broadcasts. He was a good broadcaster, for you cannot suppress a strong personality on the air, but in the early days there was not much difference between his approach as a public orator and as a private broadcaster. I remembered how back in 1935 he got overexcited while broadcasting from the studio during the passage of the India Bill. It was a subject on which he felt very strongly, and halfway through the broadcast the control room wondered what was happening when an unaccountable hammering noise started coming through the microphone. It was Churchill, pounding the table with his fist.

The first time I went to Number 10 to broadcast him, he had just taken office. This was the first time I had had to deal with him as prime minister. I arrived at Downing Street and was met by his private secretary, to whom I explained that I would have to do a voice test, a rehearsal. So along the corridor came his amazing figure, and for me it was like meeting Sir John Reith for the first time again after so many years. He had the same personality, the same overwhelming air of power. Over the years I had had experience of monarchs and princes, archbishops and more than one prime minister. But here, I felt, was a man you could not teach much.

Yet we did have a problem. Here we had a man who had to speak in one small room to a microphone and four walls, but who was used to getting up in the House of Commons and making the most of it, giving a complete performance with all the gestures, responses, echoes and audience reactions. How would he handle the changeover?

We began with a rehearsal at his usual business desk. I always tried to keep people natural and relaxed, in familiar surroundings. As always I used twin microphones, one for emergencies, and we discussed the length of the speech and how he would end. We were both rather tense on the first occasion. I left the door of the neighbouring control room open, to try and get him settled, and told him he had to wait for Big Ben, and to be announced. He turned

A World in Your Ear

on me.

'Why Big Ben?' he said. 'I am speaking. The world is waiting for *me*, not for Big Ben.'

I replied, 'Well, the world is waiting for Big Ben too, and you do have to be announced.'

He wouldn't have that either.

'Everybody will know me,' he argued.

I replied, 'Well they may not do.'

He glared at me, and I said 'Go.'

It was the best way to get him going, fighting like mad like that. After a while when he got used to the procedure he always used to have some small, last-minute panic — there would be something missing, or something he wanted, a little thing like his glasses case or a handkerchief. I remember once he had me scurrying upstairs at Chequers for his glasses, which he'd forgotten, or perhaps his watch, just a few minutes before zero. It was partly to work me up, which he didn't often succeed in doing, and partly to get himself into trim, to get the adrenalin going, so that he could sit in that small room and broadcast to the world with no reactions or responses to help him. Everyone was waiting for Churchill and he had to inspire them. That was something. It was always a marvellous performance.

It even worked with me. I would leave Merton to drive over to his home at Westerham, or to Chequers, with the feeling that things were really all over. The drive itself added to my depression since I had to fight my way through the blackout with just two tiny headlights like candles on the front of the car.

War of Words

I often used to think that the worse the night was, for weather or bombing, the more certain Churchill would be to choose it for a broadcast. But then I would listen to him speak and, when he'd finished, I would find that we hadn't had it after all, we still had a fighting chance, and come what may we were going to win. It was an extraordinary achievement.

I used to have to listen to his speeches very carefully, for he was a great one for adding a bit on at the end. He would say in rehearsal, 'This is how I'll end.' But when he was wound up he often found more to say, and heaven help me if I'd cut him off before he'd finished. So I had to watch very carefully, the door between us always left open, waiting for him to look up and signal that he was finally through. He was a devil to work for, but a treat to work with, because he made you feel Britain was getting somewhere at last.

Afterwards he liked to have a chat about things generally, and ask where I was going and how things were. We always had a drink after the broadcast, and there would be a few cigars for the journey. I still treasure one or two as mementoes. I used to have a glass of Johnny Walker Black Label whisky: I felt I needed it, and it helped me back home through the dreadful blackout. It was very difficult to get any drink during the war, but Churchill always had supplies, as he should have.

No-one else from the BBC was ever present on these occasions. Churchill would not have tolerated the presence of any producer, script editor or the like. He knew what he wanted to say and I knew how

A World in Your Ear

to broadcast it, and that was that. He surprised my wife once during the war by phoning personally to ask if I could drive over to Chequers by 5.00. 'I do like that nice young man to look after me,' he explained to my wife, who was too overcome to reply.

As time went by I became aware that Churchill, with his irrepressible sense of theatre, was starting to bring his microphones to life. The one on the right represented Hitler, the emergency microphone on the left was clearly Mussolini. As he spoke he would sneer at them and occasionally he would flick his cigar ash over the Mussolini-mike, which he obviously thoroughly despised.

When he was staying in the permanent suite he had had fitted out at the Central War Room at Storey's Gate, he invariably wore his siren suit — that was the only place he wore it. It was RAF blue, both light and warm, and he managed to look comfortable and scrupulously tidy in it. He had a private basement office-cum-bedroom there, next door to the Map Room where it was possible to see the up-to-the-minute situation on every front. More than once I had to collect him from the Map Room when we had less than three minutes to go. He was always determined that as far as military security allowed he would give his listeners the very latest information and I have seen him alter his script just as the second hand ticked to 9.00.

About this time I noticed that his script would sometimes be typed out in larger characters than the average typewriter has, like free verse; any phrase to

War of Words

which he wanted to give special emphasis stood on a line by itself. The spacing of the lines was broad and we never really knew how long the broadcast was going to take. If last-minute alterations were frequent, so were variations from the script. But he never lost his place. In all my years with radio I have never before or since seen anyone so massively composed at the microphone.

At Chequers the microphone was installed in the library, a small cosy place. When the time came for the broadcast I would find him surrounded by General Smuts, Sir Ian Fraser, Lord Beaverbrook, Brendan Bracken and Harry Hopkins, often with a cigar and a drink in his hand, and it was as hard to get him away from them as from the Map Room at Storey's Gate. No-one sat in the room with him while he spoke, but Mrs Churchill was always the first person to greet him when he had finished.

I happened to be visiting the Central War Room in the early days of the war on the occasion that Rudolf Hess, Hitler's right-hand man, dropped by parachute into Scotland on his unusual mission to meet Churchill and negotiate a settlement. The prime minister, when told of his arrival, said curtly, 'Never heard of him. Not very interested. Take good care of him.' Churchill, at least, was not ready to make peace at any price and that was the last we heard of Hess for a long time.

But I shall never forget the day the news came that the *Bismarck* had been sunk. This German battleship had played havoc with our shipping and its sinking was one of our first early successes. I was again in the

A World in Your Ear

Central War Room at the time, and Churchill's jubilation on hearing the news was incredible. When the RAF went in and disabled the monster, he very nearly swung from the chandeliers in delight; he was in ecstasy.

There was another amusing incident one day when he was about to carry out a special broadcast from 10 Downing Street. He suddenly stopped, frowned and looked around; the ticking of a beautiful antique clock on the mantelpiece was annoying him. He glared at the thing: it went tick, tock, tick, tock — as it had, with faultless precision, for hundreds of years. 'Stop that damn thing,' he ordered. 'It sounds like bloody jackboots, and I won't have them marching in Downing Street.'

I shot over to the mantelpiece, but the clock had been built to last and, though I fiddled with the works, I couldn't stop it. A glare from Churchill, however, encouraged me to try less gentle methods, and eventually I managed to silence it. I should be surprised if it ever worked again.

Churchill was not the only important person to broadcast at this busy period. In the early days of the war, when we were looking for allies, the American ambassador in London decided to broadcast his views on the state of Britain to his people back home. Ambassador Joseph Kennedy, father of President Kennedy, had a house at Winkfield Road, Windsor, which he used for entertaining of one kind and another, quite apart from playing host to the diplomatic community. I was sent down there to

War of Words

arrange his broadcast with my old friend Fred Bate and Ed Murrow, later one of the most famous American commentators. Some time after the first rehearsal, Fred and I suddenly realized that the time for the broadcast was coming up and we had lost the ambassador and Mr Murrow. Searching along the corridors, I finally pushed open a door and found Mr Kennedy and Mr Murrow had joined in a noisy party that was taking place and were not overconcerned about the broadcast ahead. But I was more horrified by what he said than by his behaviour, for he told America that in his view Britain did not have a chance and was finished.

As luck would have it, I happened to be at Buckingham Palace the next evening and mentioned the ambassador's speech to the king's private secretary. The broadcast had been recorded only for the American networks, not for transmission to Britain, but I felt that Kennedy's defeatist views were significant to London too. I think my hint was followed and the broadcast listened to, for Kennedy was recalled to the United States shortly afterwards and replaced by the charming and efficient Ambassador Hudson.

In the early days of the war I was also busy with a series of technical problems. I had been assigned the task of setting up a network of small regional transmitters. It had been decided at a very high level that in the event of an invasion it would be wise to erect a number of low-power transmitter units, scattered around the country. They were known as the H-group

A World in Your Ear

and had a radius of ten miles or so. They could be operated by the local authorities or zone commanders to broadcast special bulletins and instructions if necessary. It did not seem improbable in those early days, with most of Europe overrun and America still an observer, that the German army could land in Britain and part of the country fall to occupying forces. In these circumstances local radio, telling people what was really happening and what to do, would be essential.

There was also the problem that even without an invasion, we were still forced to close down each high-power transmitter if there was an air-raid alert in its area, so that enemy planes could not use it to get their bearings. This meant that parts of the country were cut off from radio for quite long periods at times of stress, with considerable anxiety and loss of morale. But the new low-power transmitters did not have to close down unless enemy aircraft were within a few miles of them, and in this way, even during the most wide-scale air raids of the 1940s, the system never broke down. Services were maintained at a reasonably high level, and the listener with an average receiver was seldom prevented from hearing BBC programmes, however unpleasantly close an air raid might have been.

I was asked to establish these sites during lulls in my everyday activities — which still included sporting events, functions and VIP broadcasts. I would start by ringing up the appropriate town clerk to make a confidential appointment, asking him to have his senior engineer and his clerk of works on hand too. I could not explain the reason over the phone, of course. Then I would travel by train or car to meet them, and explain what we were planning and what we needed.

We tried to site the transmitters on council property wherever possible, to avoid having to explain to a private landlord what we were doing. We also needed a suitable building nearby to attach the aerial to, plus reasonable clearance so that its surroundings did not interfere with our transmission and so that we had easy access.

We found ourselves making do in a strange variety of situations. In Scarborough, for instance, I found the best site was the Poor Law Institution. There was nowhere our engineers could be accommodated, so we had to erect our own blast-protected surface shelter, but the institution did provide lavatory and toilet facilities, which were often something of a luxury, and a mobile catering unit which we could call on if the need arose.

At a number of other places, such as Oxford, I decided the council water tower would prove a satisfactory home for our transmitter. This was the case at Luton, though there the council's tower stood on land belonging to a Major Harrison. But he gave us permission to use it, and to attach a mast to his own private tower too, so we could run an aerial between the two. At Blackpool we established ourselves in the Derby swimming baths, which were new and luckily built of substantially reinforced concrete; we found ourselves a couple of rooms in the basement and attached our mast to the main chimney stack.

At York we moved our transmitter into the basement of the Yorkshire Museum. There was nowhere suitable to attach the aerial, so we had to build a mast, but luckily York is fairly flat and the site was ideal. At Shrewsbury we found a safe place in the basement of Shrewsbury Castle which had a heavy flagstone floor, massive oak beams in the ceiling and walls seven feet thick. We ran our aerial from the top of the Laura Tower down the hill to the castle itself. At Peterborough we moved into the Park Laundry in Park Road, owned by a Mr H. Butcher. Mr Butcher was away on active service, but the town clerk was an old friend of his and he let us borrow his friend's premises, which had a convenient 60-foot chimney stack.

Other sites were less well endowed. At Swindon we had to start from scratch on a bare site; at Sheffield we had to move into a partially-blitzed school; at Reading we used the People's Pantry, in the centre of town, which had recently been bought by the council as a centre for the communal feeding of evacuees.

In every case it was a question of going round with the town clerk as soon as I had arrived and explained my mission, looking either for some sort of tall building to attach my aerial to, or for a substantially-built place to house the transmitter safe from raids — or, if possible, both, close together. We could always rig up an aerial mast, or build a blast-proof shelter, but it was obviously quicker and cheaper and better not to have to build both.

Ipswich was one place that posed problems at first. It did not possess many large industrial chimney stacks, as most of the brick and tile works for which the town was famous were no longer active, and were in any case situated a considerable way from any power supply. But in the end we were able to put the transmitter into the basement of the St Matthew's swimming baths, which were already bomb-proof, and to fit the aerial to the roof. I found the council people in Ipswich particularly helpful, and delighted that some effort was being made to help reception there, which they assured me was very poor. Their friendliness compensated me a little for my dreadful journey there; I had driven through east London in the middle of an all-out air raid, with bombs dropping, buildings crashing down and sirens wailing along the deserted streets, and I felt lucky to have reached Ipswich in one piece.

We started in 1940, when we were already frantically busy, being short-staffed, and all these visits to set up the local transmitters had to be completed in detail on the spot. In one day I would survey the site, get the council surveyor to draw up a plan, appoint the building and electrical contractors and the steeplejacks, visit the landlord if it was not council property and fix a rent (usually in the nature of £30 a year), draw up the costs and a timetable — and be back in my office within 24 hours. We had the first ten low-power transmitters in operation by November 1940, and more followed in 1941; in the end we had

A World in Your Ear

put 60 of them into service.

My family and I spent all the war years in London. In my case there was no option. As the war progressed, the various parts of the BBC were dispersed to safer venues around the country — the variety department went to Bangor, North Wales, the research department to Droitwich and so on. But mine was last on the list. When the prime minister and the monarch left, then I could go. And, since the king had no intention of leaving London, come what might, and Churchill wouldn't hear of it either, I was stuck too, as were my family. By this time my children were at secondary school, my son at Raynes Park County School and my daughter at Mitcham High School, both trying to work normally despite the circumstances.

It was a strange situation, trying to lead a normal life in an abnormal situation, and sometimes you did crazy things. I remember one afternoon late in 1940. It was a Saturday or Sunday, and for once I had come home before dark. It was a beautiful day and I was out working in the garden when we heard a zurr, zurr, zurr. Right in the distance, looking east from my garden, we could see a formation of aeroplanes. All of a sudden I realized it was a formation of German bombers and we were in for a raid. Next thing, we heard bang, bang, bang: our boys were up there among them.

The battle was all happening in the sky above Croydon, and when, suddenly, the sky cleared I turned to my son Bill and said, 'Let's drive over and see it.' And off we went. I don't know what made me do it: we didn't find anything to see and we could both have been killed. It was just that, for that one time, it was as though it was all a stage performance for us to watch, not a real event. It was so clear and beautiful and eerie to stand in your own back garden and watch the war.

But sometimes the raids came nearer, and then we had to take shelter in a Morrison-type shelter in the living room. More often still, the raids came while I was away, and I would go about my job in town wondering and worrying about my wife and children at home. Barbara did not always know where I was, because sometimes when I had to go out to the country I could not tell her my destination on the telephone. Merton was not a good spot. It was too near Croydon, which was heavily attacked at that time. And Mitcham was in the line of approach for the Battle of Britain: we often saw our planes going over. But fortunately we were never hit; one just got used to the thump, thump, thump.

By late 1940 we were beginning to feel that Britain was getting somewhere at last in this war. I did a broadcast from Trafalgar Square with Ed Murrow that tried to give his American listeners a picture of what it was like to be in London during an air raid. I set up my effects microphones outside in the square, and he did his commentary from the crypt of St Martin's-in-the-Fields, the great church that stands on its east side. We were lucky to have lots of action that night, for the Germans kindly decided to blitz central London and all hell was let loose. This broadcast,

A World in Your Ear

coming before Pearl Harbor, helped I think better than anything else to convey to the American people the picture of London at war. It showed just what we were up against, what London was going through night after night, and it was appreciated by many people who had visited the capital and could imagine the scene. But this was a difficult period. Many a time I could hardly get back to the office through the damaged streets, and then Broadcasting House itself was hit and for three days I had to use my car, parked outside, as an office.

Steadily, throughout the war, I was asked to set up a series of high-level broadcasts, not only by the king and the prime minister, but also by foreign dignitaries who had found refuge in Britain. Sometimes they came to the microphone to tell the British people what had happened in their countries, but more often the broadcasts were beamed abroad so they could tell their compatriots that Britain was still fighting, and that it was important to continue harassing the German occupation forces and to keep up their spirits, their hopes and their opposition. This was a propaganda war and they all had their part to play. I recorded Princess Marina at Coppins, and Queen Wilhelmina of Holland and King Haakon VII of Norway from Buckingham Palace. I would go and rehearse them first, using a copy of the script with a red mark where they were to stop. Unlike Sir Winston, they had to stop where they had indicated, with no ad-libbing, because I could not speak their languages and could not listen for extra remarks.

War of Words

Queen Wilhelmina of the Netherlands broadcast in July 1940 and was accommodated at Buckingham Palace for a while. Later her daughter, the present Queen Juliana, arrived too, with her husband Prince Bernhard. They all made themselves at home, and I remember George VI remarking to me on one occasion, looking round at this influx of foreign cousins at the palace, that he wondered where *he* was going to sleep that night!

Queen Wilhelmina always reminded me of Queen Victoria, she had such a keen eye for ceremony and dignity and what she thought to be her due. It was not always easy to persuade these foreign monarchs of the need to rehearse their broadcasts in advance, to check on voice levels and suchlike. Queen Wilhelmina of Romania arrived and did a broadcast to try and rally her people, which I also arranged. She was given a large house just outside Cambridge, for Buckingham Palace by this time was bursting.

I arranged broadcasting facilities at a moment's notice for any allied government from wherever they wanted. A number of foreign generals, ambassadors and other notables broadcast from the Central War Room: the ether was loaded with calls for resistance. Even our own queen made one of her rare broadcasts on 14 June 1940 when she spoke in French to the women of France to rally them to our cause.

One regular broadcaster who made his first broadcast in June 1940 was General de Gaulle. He had come from France with what French troops he could muster and Churchill was giving him his right hand to

A World in Your Ear

support him. De Gaulle was rather a stiff, rigid figure, not easy to get along with. But Churchill and he respected each other, each, I think, recognizing the other's quality. They had the measure of each other.

I was at Chequers once, preparing for a broadcast, and Churchill was waiting for de Gaulle whom he'd invited to lunch. It was a bad, foggy day and Chequers, as I knew well, was a difficult place to find in bad weather, with its approach largely concealed. Churchill was a devil for being prompt, but he waited and waited and I saw the clock ticking on, and in the end he just said, 'Lunch will be served,' and started his meal. De Gaulle arrived considerably late, for his driver had indeed taken the wrong road, and he came in and looked very affronted when he saw that Churchill had begun. Churchill just said, 'Well, when I say luncheon I mean luncheon,' and was quite unrepentant.

In 1941 I found myself a more light-hearted assignment. Hubert Tannar, the headmaster of the Royal School at Windsor, which catered for the children whose parents worked on the royal estates, was a great enthusiast for amateur theatricals. So he was enlisted by Princess Elizabeth and Princess Margaret to help them put on a Christmas pantomime at Windsor. They had staged a simple nativity play the year before and enjoyed it enormously. Now they wanted to extend their range.

Mr Tannar leapt to the challenge and wrote a splendid script which starred Princess Elizabeth as Prince Charming and her younger sister as Cinderella.

War of Words

Then they started looking around for some professional advisers. I found myself telephoned by the superintendent of Windsor Castle, at the request of the princesses, to assist them with sound distribution and microphone technique for the pantomime. Profits from the show, to be staged in the Waterloo Chamber of the castle, were to go to the war fund for charity.

So on a number of afternoons I slipped away from my desk, went down to Windsor and set up my microphones and loudspeakers so the show could be heard easily all over the chamber. It was great fun, and the only uneasy moment came at the end of the show when Mr Tannar, rather overcome by the success of the venture and the audience's applause, kept on bowing and bowing and looked as though he would never leave the stage. On impulse I picked up a record of the Flying Scotsman, which we were using for sound effects, slammed it on to the turntable and let it thunder out over the loudspeakers, wheels, whistle and all. Mr Tannar shot off the stage like a startled deer and the show collapsed in laughter. It became something of a joke with the royal family after that, and they would confess to me sometimes after a particularly long state function, 'We could have done with the Flying Scotsman!'

The pantomimes were a welcome break and cheered everyone up. The following year they did *Aladdin*, followed by *Old Mother Red Riding Boots*, a haphazard mixture of half a dozen traditional pantomime stories. One pleasant touch introduced by Princess Elizabeth when she was arranging the latter

A World in Your Ear

was to cover the walls with pantomime pictures. The great oil paintings commemorating the Napoleonic wars that usually hung in the Waterloo Chamber — portraits of George III and George IV, the Duke of Wellington and Field Marshal von Blücher, Alexander I of Russia, Francis I of Austria, Prince Metternich and various generals — these had been taken to a safer place for fear of damage. In their place Princess Elizabeth hung oil paintings of Aladdin, Mother Goose and Cinderella in the elaborate gilt frames. They certainly made the room more cheerful for the pantomimes. When the war ended and the pictures were returned to the Waterloo Chamber, King George VI decided that they should be placed back in their frames over the pantomime portraits, so that a secret vestige of those happy days remains, hidden from sightseers.

Another happy occasion at Windsor was when we took the complete cast of ITMA there. King George VI loved this comedy programme, and nothing was allowed to interrupt while Tommy Handley and his brilliant cast were on the air. So he decided to call a Royal Command Performance of ITMA for Princess Elizabeth's birthday in 1942. Francis Worsley, the show's producer, went with me and the whole ITMA team to Windsor. It was a doubly complicated event for me, for it had been decided to broadcast the show, so I had to set up microphones for the recording as well as for the live performance. But it went off successfully and it was a pleasure to see the king enjoying himself so much.

War of Words

I always felt it was part of my job to be conversant on many subjects when I was with the royal family, to help put them at their ease and not leave all the strain of making conversation to them. People, even supposedly high-ranking and intelligent people at the BBC, used to say to me sometimes, 'What do you do when the king speaks to you?' To which I could only make the obvious reply: 'I speak to him back, of course.' Did they think I stood there dumb? One thing I always did when talking to the king and queen was try to bring something extra to the conversation. For instance, if I chatted to them after one of the pantomimes, I didn't just say what a marvellous show it had been and leave it at that — they had been there themselves after all and had their own opinions. So I would say something like, 'I thought I'd never get here tonight, the weather's so awful and the blackout's so thick.' And they would ask me about it: they liked to know what was going on all the time. Particularly during the war, the king and queen were always most anxious to know how the man in the street was getting on, how people managed and whether they could bear it much longer. The king never forgot what he had to do. His two daughters, if things had got extreme, might have been moved. But never he or the queen; they would stay till the end.

But peace came at last. Winston Churchill broadcast triumphantly to the nation on VE Day, 8 May 1945 and King George VI broadcast from Buckingham Palace in the evening. We were going back to normal.

6

Festival and coronation

Before the final victory came, later that year, there was a general election and Clement Atlee succeeded Churchill as prime minister. He was a kind, intelligent man. He had been a marvellous deputy to Churchill throughout the war and he became a great peacetime leader. He spoke from 10 Downing Street on the evening that the final victory was announced, surrounded by his stalwarts Ernest Bevin, Herbert Morrison and others.

Champagne was served, and I thought it was typical of Attlee's sense of honour that after the first toast, 'To victory', he immediately proposed his second toast, 'To an absent leader'. We were all aware of the shadow of the absent Churchill, and I thought this was a very fine gesture. But there was no time to brood. I had the king's broadcast to arrange, and a massive victory parade to prepare coverage for. We had returned to our usual hectic routine.

As usual we were very short of both equipment and money. But I heard of a sale of government surplus radio equipment in Gamages department store at Holborn and managed to pick up a considerable amount of stuff, out of which I was able to rig up the

Festival and coronation

things we needed. One interesting venture was the fitting out for broadcasting of *HMS Campaign*. King George VI and Attlee had launched a campaign under the slogan 'Britain can make it' and we were all trying to encourage initiative, self-confidence and a return to normality. *HMS Campaign* was a sea-borne exhibition which travelled from port to port to demonstrate what could be done, and an outside broadcasting engineer was permanently on board.

In 1946 I also met a man who was to become the king's private secretary and a great and valued personal friend of mine. This was Major Michael Adeane, now Lord Adeane. In a most unassuming way, he was a perfectionist in all matters. His great interest in outside broadcasts gave me a reassuring feeling of support and helped me break new ground. For it was soon agreed that I could arrange sound recordings of the state banquets at Buckingham Palace, and from then on I was installed, alone, in the orchestral gallery with my control equipment overlooking the glittering dinner table below; the commentary was ghosted in at Broadcasting House.

A little of that glitter was soon to come my way. I was inspecting my incoming mail in my office at 55 Portland Place on 4 December 1945 when my secretary handed me a white envelope marked 'OHMS'. Wondering what assignment this was going to be, I found inside a letter from the prime minister marked 'Urgent — personal and confidential'. It was a formal letter from my friend Leslie Rowan, Mr Attlee's private secretary, telling me of the prime minister's intention of submitting my name to George VI with a recommendation for an MBE. I was overcome for a few minutes, thinking of my reply. The recommendation had been submitted to Downing Street by the BBC, of course; I wrote to Number 10 accepting, and conveyed my thanks to the director-general's office.

Two weeks later, on 18 December, I was again in my office when I was handed an even larger envelope with the royal cypher on it, also marked 'Confidential'. Inside was a formal letter from Sir Ulick Alexander, secretary of the Royal Victorian Order, stating the king's intention of appointing me a member of the order. The MVO is unique because it is the only British honour bestowed personally by the monarch for services rendered to him; for all other decorations he accepts the recommendations of parliament. I was nonplussed — and this time the BBC congratulated me.

January 1946 arrived, and I was invited to Buckingham Palace, as my name had appeared in the New Year's honours list. It was the first time I had gone there without a microphone. The decoration was bestowed on me during a private audience with the king. He began by saying, 'Now I'm going to do the talking this time and you'll be doing the listening.' I was, for once, terribly nervous; I could say very little, but listened mesmerized while the king recounted my endeavours. I heard no more about the MBE; the BBC obviously felt that one honour was quite enough for me.

With the war behind us, outside broadcasts began

Festival and coronation

to return to the old pattern. The big band broadcasts of old had gone, because restaurants could no longer afford to employ them in these days of rationing and austerity, so now the bands came to the studio. But we were still taking excerpts from theatres, and sometimes did a complete relay from a musical like *Oklahoma* or *Annie Get Your Gun* — marvellous shows that really excited people.

There was also plenty of sport: cricket and football, race meetings and boxing. A number of commentators made their names in sports — Eamonn Andrews, who began as a boxing commentator, the excellent Raymond Glendenning, and Howard Marshall, the first of the great ceremonial commentators, whose coverage of the Duke of Kent's wedding in 1934 had set the standard for royal occasions. He was a marvellously flexible broadcaster who began the hard way covering the TT motorbike races in the Isle of Man, and Irish race meetings.

At the end of 1946 we covered the departure of *HMS Vanguard* carrying the king, queen and the two princesses to South Africa. The winter of 1947 which followed was one of the worst Britain had ever experienced. But when the *Vanguard* returned it was a warm sunny day in Southampton, with bands playing and troops everywhere. The vessel slowly pulled in alongside her docking position and I was beside our outside broadcasting control van, standing next to Richard Dimbleby, the commentator. Suddenly two figures appeared on the bridge: the king and queen had come out to watch. A few minutes

A World in Your Ear

later the queen waved her hand and I waved back enthusiastically. Then the king waved, and poor old Richard Dimbleby wondered just what was going to happen next!

Soon after this I was at the Guildhall where the king and queen were guests of honour at a function. As the queen came past she said to me, 'It was so nice to see you when we arrived back from Africa — you were one of the first friends we saw.' The assumption of friendship was a compliment I treasured.

But it reflected, I think, a genuine feeling on the part of the king and queen that after all the years we had worked together, we did have a special relationship. I remember a couple of incidents that showed this clearly. On one occasion the king's private secretary said to me as I was leaving after a visit to the palace, 'Come with me, I've something that will interest you.' He led me into a private room and left me there with the casual remark: 'Shut the door as you leave.' I looked about me and was dazzled by some of the most marvellous crown regalia. Here were all the private jewels of the king and queen, the brooches and tiaras and necklaces, the glittering swords and sets of gold, set out on display around this strongroom and worth more than I could imagine. The degree of trust that allowed me to wander around and explore the treasure on my own was a touching demonstration of my privileged position in the household. On another occasion a newcomer to the palace administration stopped me as I was going through a door, and the king's equerry, seeing what

Festival and coronation

had happened, called out, 'Oh, that's Mr Wood. He's all right — he's one of the family.'

Two events made 1947 notable for me. It was the year in which I invented the first 22-inch parabolic microphone reflector using a moving-coil microphone and a reflector dish. This enhanced the pick-up of very remote sound-effects like street noises, fireworks or distant conversations. I received a merit award for my effort, which was picked up at once not only by the BBC but by the newsreel companies; but, alas, no patent was granted and I received no royalty.

The other event recalled the early days for me. Sir William Haley, the current director-general, invited me to a dinner at Claridges on 19 November 1947 in honour of Lord Reith and in celebration of the BBC's silver jubilee. It was a sign of those difficult times, however, that I had another letter shortly afterwards saying the venue had been changed to the council chamber of Broadcasting House because of a hotel strike.

That month I was in control in the abbey for the wedding of Princess Elizabeth and Prince Philip. This caused me no problems, because the microphone dispostion was the same as for the Duke of Kent's marriage to Princess Marina in 1934. As I've said before, cathedral acoustics don't change; nor of course does the wedding service. Worldwide reports of the broadcast were good.

A special set of the whole BBC recording was made and sent to Buckingham Palace, for the royal family had not heard the commentary themselves since they

A World in Your Ear

were all in the abbey. But the king told me he did not have a good record reproducer. Within a week I designed and made a reproducer in our workshop from the best components then available, which was mounted in a nice cabinet by the BBC carpenters. I demonstrated this to the director-general and the chief engineer in his suite before taking it along to Buckingham Palace. The king and queen were delighted, and the unit went with them to Sandringham and was well used by the royal family over the holidays. I heard the results of my work many times, for the king was quite an expert disc-jockey, and in fact very well versed mechanically and electrically. He was very much the all-round engineer of the royal family, with considerable know-how. During the war he had a room at Windsor equipped for him where he could precision-finish various gun mechanisms by hand. He liked doing this very much and often asked me to obtain certain small tool items for him, which I did.

A year after Lord Reith, I had my own celebration. On 23 July 1948 I received a letter congratulating me on my 25 years with the corporation. Six days later came a new challenge: coverage of all outside broadcasts for the Olympic Games, held that time in England. The 14th Olympic Games put a huge strain on our resources. Everything was still being done on a shoe-string, but now — used to all that radio could do — people expected more and more of us, unaware of the technical shortages we faced. 61 countries competed in the games, which we hoped would shake

Festival and coronation

off the taint of Nazism that had infected the last Olympics, held in Berlin under Hitler. Political newcomers had begun to join us, and among the names we grew familiar with were Afghanistan, Cuba, Iran, Iraq, Korea and Lichtenstein.

The games had been held in Britain only once before, in 1908. (Then there had been no radio coverage. In 1948 there was hardly any television coverage, and at least I was free of what little there was: when television services were resumed after the war they were assigned their own outside-broadcasting unit, to my very great relief.) I was responsible for all the outside venues — Aldershot (modern pentathlon and equestrian events), Bisley (rifle shooting), Camberley (modern pentathlon and equestrian), Finchley (water polo), Harringay (basketball), Henley (rowing ands canoeing), Herne Hill (the cycling centre), Windsor Great Park (the road cycle race), the Guinness, Lyons and London Polytechnic hockey fields, and Arsenal, Crystal Palace, Fulham, Ilford, Brentford, Dulwich, Tottenham and Walthamstow football grounds for all the qualifying games in the Olympic football series.

At this time another idea was taking hold in Attlee's mind. His whole theme was that Britain could make it, and he wanted to show the people that this was indeed possible, and demonstrate to them their present achievements as a way of encouraging them to do even more. He hit on the idea of a Festival of Britain, to be held on the centenary of Queen Victoria's Great Exhibition and to be a similar declaration of faith. My task was to organize complete radio coverage of the South Bank exhibition and the Festival Gardens, and to cover the jubilee wedding celebrations of the king and queen, which coincided very happily with the exhibition.

I shall never forget the evening when the king and queen made a joint broadcast to the nation at 9.00 from Buckingham Palace following a state drive south of the Thames. The streets were full of cheering people, and from 8.00 I was pacing the floor at the palace waiting anxiously for them to arrive. Time ticked on and I began to get really worried. By 8.50 there was still no sign of them. Broadcasting House was getting into a terrible flap — and so was I.

Finally, with just a few minutes to spare, the coach drove in at the sovereign's entrance, the king and queen dashed up the stairs, and on went the red light. There were only a couple of seconds in hand, and no time for a rehearsal, but by now the king was such an excellent broadcaster he didn't need one. Queen Elizabeth told me afterwards that they had been held up by enthusiastic crowds all along the route, and it was only as they were coming over Westminster Bridge and saw Big Ben that they noticed it was already 8.45. 'I said, "Mr Wood will be so worried — we must get on," ' and so they had urged the coach on, their concern for other people's problems coming foremost in their minds as usual.

That year ended with another high spot for me. On 4 December 1951 I was made a Freeman of the City of London. I'd covered the Lord Mayor's Banquet

Festival and coronation

year after year since about 1926. The banquet is always regarded as an important occasion since the prime minister of the day is the guest of honour, and usually seizes the occasion to make an important statement, so there was always some titbit coming out of it and it was always recorded. I was proud and delighted to be made a Freeman, because I think London is the most important city in the world — and I've worked all over it. It was in the mayoralty of Sir Howard Leslie Boyce KBE, and I accepted gratefully.

We had something of a return to old times later that year, when Winston Churchill resumed office as prime minister. He broadcast for the first time that session from the ground floor of Chartwell, where he had made so many broadcasts in the past, and I felt, 'Well, the old man is back where he belongs.' Since then I've had a run of them. Eden, I thought, made a marvellous foreign secretary, but I never found him convincing as a prime minister. Macmillan was a remarkable man. He put you at ease immediately; there was no fuss, no bother. He liked the microphone. He was leisurely and relaxed, and marvellous as a host to people like President Eisenhower — a wonderful diplomat and an ideal gentleman of peace. But he was succeeded by Sir Alec Douglas-Home and although I had only a short experience of him, I did not find him convincing either. Churchill was a different figure — although he was growing old: he had his first stroke leaving the abbey after the coronation in 1953.

He was, however, one of the few dignitaries I met

who managed to approach my wife. She always preferred to keep in the background, and although, now that the children were grown up, she often came with me down to Westerham in the 1950s when Churchill was again prime minister, she preferred to sit in the car reading a book while she waited for me to finish. On one occasion Churchill's private secretary went out to invite her inside. It was not the first invitation, but as usual she was too shy and she declined. However, the secretary was persistent and in the end she agreed, very nervously.

She was waiting for me when the prime minister arrived at his study for the broadcast. From where I was checking my equipment I heard that unmistakable hearty voice asking, 'Who is this lady?' I heard his secretary explain and heard Churchill stride off towards her.

When I went to collect Barbara after the broadcast, there was no sign of her. Searching around I found the secretary, who explained that Sir Winston had come straight round to her after the broadcast, while I was packing my equipment away, and had persuaded her to go on a tour of his paintings: he was a most enthusiastic painter and loved to show off the work in his studio. They were gone over half an hour, and, once she got over the shock, Barbara, like everyone else, warmed to his friendly company.

It was getting harder and harder to do anything new in outside broadcasting, for by now we had tried everything. But we had a nice challenge in 1951, when BEA launched a regular London to Paris service

Festival and coronation

which took less than an hour's flying time. We decided to take listeners on one of these flights. Richard Dimbleby was the BBC's man on board and I arranged the coverage. The plane took off from Heathrow at 8.00 and we broadcast continuously. On board I installed a transmitter and receiver, and we had six reception points on the ground to pick up the signals as the plane crossed over — three in England and three in France. We had an engineer on the plane and the transmission was passed from station to station as they flew across. I had to make sure each reception point overlapped with the preceding one so there was no danger of a poor signal at any point. Since the Channel is blessedly level, with no interference from hazards like mountains or tall buildings, we were able to cover two-thirds of it from the British side and two-thirds from the French side, so we didn't need to set up a reception point in the Channel itself.

We had commentators stationed at various places to talk to Dimbleby as he flew overhead. He took off promptly at 8.00 and described the take-off, the dinner as it was served en route and the landscape as he flew over, and he chatted to the commentators on the ground. At one and a half minutes to 9.00, he landed at Le Bourget. It was quite an innovation, this two-way commentary from an aircraft, put out live, with the listener feeling he was on board and kept in the picture all the way. It was done during the summer, at a nice time of the evening, and was a very pleasant little broadcast.

A World in Your Ear

But not every outside broadcast went off as smoothly as this for, in the nature of things, there was always the totally unexpected to expect! A nerve-racking experience happened one Boat Race day in the mid-1950s. It was a nice spring Saturday morning when the phone went and the late Geoffrey Peck, one of our top sports commentators, told me that our launch had slipped its moorings in the night and was lying on the mud flats down river with all our equipment on board. We had carried out a trial run of the course the day before, and left everything in order, and now we faced disaster.

We made off for Putney at once and the worst was confirmed on arrival. What could we do? While I cudgelled my brains, my wife said, 'Couldn't your friends at Wapping, the river police, help?' What an inspiration! I phoned them from the landing stage and begged for assistance, and they said they would do all they could. My engineers and I waited and waited, our hearts in our mouths. Then, through the centre archway of Putney Bridge, there appeared a fully-manned police launch with all our equipment safe and sound. In a very short time we were installed on board and testing. Believe me, we looked really smart and well protected when we followed the crews 'in line' on that memorable day. It was a wonderful gesture and effort on their part, and one that I will never forget. And it brought it home to me again that in outside broadcasting you have to react fast and try any way, however unorthodox or irregular, of keeping on the air.

Festival and coronation

The end of 1951 was marked by the saddest broadcast of my career. King George VI had been gravely ill and had had a lung operation. He still wished to do the traditional Christmas broadcast live, but the queen felt it would be impossible. One day she asked me in confidence to go along to the palace to record it. It was the first and only time it had been recorded. The king didn't like recordings — he didn't agree with them at all, for he felt strongly that he should make the effort to talk directly to his people. But the operations had tired him so much, and his throat was so strained, that it was impossible.

I had to disappear discreetly from my office, so I took home, the night before, some second-rate commercial recording equipment which I'd had to borrow unobserved from our mobile recording department. I never used recording equipment — everything I did was live, all the time — and I could not have explained what it was intended for if anyone had asked me what I was doing. I took it home to modify and improve it, and carried it over to Buckingham Palace the following afternoon.

King George VI and Queen Elizabeth were waiting in the Sunshine Room at the palace, which was our usual broadcasting room, and I started recording. As soon as the king heard the playback of the first words, he realized how impossible it would have been for him to broadcast live. He went through the speech just a few words at a time, resting in between. It took a very long time, at least two hours, before the few hundred words were finally complete; it was very,

very distressing for him and the queen, and for me, because I admired him so much and wished I could do more to help.

Then I went back to 55 Portland Place and locked myself away in the basement and started to transfer the recording on to disc. I had to transcribe it in snatches, making sure the voice levels matched exactly and there were no awkward jumps or gaps. Ironically, there was a big outside broadcast Christmas party going on upstairs on the fourth floor, with people like Dimbleby and all the top brass in attendance. I'd absented myself from the office that afternoon without being able to explain why, and now I was staying away from the party, for only the director-general and the very senior chief engineer knew what I was involved in, toiling away in the basement. I'm afraid I lost a lot of goodwill among my colleagues that day.

Finally I finished and took the disc home — there was nowhere secure to leave it at Broadcasting House at that hour of the night. The next day I brought it in with me and it went under lock and key till it was time for the broadcast. The king heard a playback beforehand, and was well pleased with it. I listened at home on Christmas Day and it brought back sad memories of that afternoon. But I sent a message to the royal family straight after the broadcast to say that it had come over well, and got a telegram back that evening from the king and queen, thanking me for the work I'd done.

King George VI died two months later in February

Festival and coronation

1952. It was decided that the funeral would follow the same pattern as that of his father, George V, and I was to be in control of the broadcast from St George's Chapel in Windsor Castle. It was quickly arranged, and I was in my office discussing the plans with my colleagues when a message came through from the director-general's office. The Queen Mother, as she now was, had requested my presence in the Garter Stalls as a guest of the royal family at the funeral service.

I hardly knew how to reply. I could scarcely refuse the invitation, which touched me deeply, but I tried to explain to the earl marshal's office that I would be there anyway, at the master microphone control panels in the vestry. In the end it was accepted that I should be present, doing my job, and could pay my respects afterwards. This broadcast was not something I wished to entrust to anyone else. I had handled all King George VI's other broadcasts and wanted, in loyalty, to stay with him to the end.

Later the same evening a motorcyclist arrived at my home in Merton with a large black-edged envelope containing permits, a seat on the special train from Paddington to Windsor and my Garter Stall permit. And, after the broadcast was over, I did indeed stay on alone in Windsor Chapel and pay my homage and remembrance to the king, alone and in my own fashion.

A year later I was back in the thick of it, organizing sound coverage of the coronation of Queen Elizabeth II. I sent my clean sound to the BBC domestic, over-

A World in Your Ear

seas and Commonwealth services, to the French, Dutch, Belgian, German and Danish radio networks, and across the Atlantic to the United States, to Central and Latin America and to Canada in both English and French. We also fed my sound to loudspeakers all along the coronation route and to the BBC commentators in the crowd.

Although it had a bigger viewing and listening audience, from my point of view it was a lot easier than the 1937 coronation. For one thing, I had done it all before, but my equipment was now much more advanced. Also, there was to be only one crowning, not two, so the ceremony was shorter and simpler. And of course this time I had a TV monitor screen at my side so I knew where everyone was all the time without relying on memory. I handled all the sound from the abbey for both radio and television, and afterwards the ITA sent me a pleasant letter of thanks for the sound I had provided to the commercial channel. The queen broadcast that evening from the same room in Buckingham Palace and at the same time as her father had in 1937, and once again I was there.

She also took up the tradition of speaking to the Commonwealth on Christmas Day. She had broadcast on a number of occasions as princess and was quite confident. I had met her several times, and been present at her first-ever broadcast on 13 October 1940 when she was 14. It was a three-minute broadcast to the children of the empire on 'Children's Hour' and at the end she made her famous impromptu

Festival and coronation

addition of saying 'Come on Margaret,' and made her younger sister, sitting at her side, join her in the 'Goodnight children'. Her first broadcast as queen was rehearsed in the normal way: the Queen Mother and the Duke of Edinburgh were there, with Sir Michael Adeane and myself.

To my dismay, the royal family were now back to the usual Sandringham Christmas holiday, and that meant my travelling down the day before. At first the queen tried to continue broadcasting live. But in 1957, the silver jubilee of the first Christmas Day broadcast, it was decided to televise the speech too, and this made problems.

With George VI, as with Churchill, there had just been the king and me; we did not need anyone else. But television seemed to demand not just a cameraman and a lighting technician, with me handling the sound for both, but also a producer, a script editor and various inexplicable assistants. There was scarcely accommodation in Sandringham village for the great crowd of people who had suddenly become involved. Two years later the queen decided to record the Christmas message in advance at Buckingham Palace, because she was expecting her third child and wanted to have a Christmas free of worry. She had echoed privately what her father felt, about the broadcast being an ordeal, and there was no doubt that the coming of television with its horde of hangers-on made the intrusion into the privacy of Sandringham all the greater. So recording became the procedure, and at last I was able to have my Christmas dinner at

A World in Your Ear

home on Christmas Day.

I made another personal and very happy recording with the queen in July 1958. She was to attend the sixth British, Empire and Commonwealth Games which were being held in Cardiff that year. She found she was unable to go, and late one evening I was called to Buckingham Palace with instructions to install recording equipment. The queen wanted to record a speech for the closing ceremony, and as I listened I heard the news for the first time that she intended to create the nine-year-old Prince Charles Prince of Wales.

Very few copies of the disc were cut, for security was very important, and I carried the recording down to Cardiff myself. The announcement was played to the crowd over the stadium's public address system at the closing ceremony and broadcast to the world from the stadium's control room at the same time. It met with great enthusiasm from the huge crowd of spectators.

The later months of 1958 were overshadowed for me by personal tragedy. My two children were now grown up; my daughter had married and moved away, my son still lived at home. He worked as a draughtsman at the Central Electricity Board and spent most of his spare time as an officer with the Air Training Corps. But he fell ill, and though he was treated for fibrositis, the trouble persisted. It must have worried me more than I thought showed, for one day the queen's private secretary, Sir Michael Adeane, asked me what was on my mind. I explained about my son's

Festival and coronation

illness and he said at once that he would try and do something. Two days later we received a telephone call telling us to make an appointment at the London Clinic.

The clinic's staff were immediately efficient and helpful, and carried out all the necessary tests on Bill. But in the end they called us into the office and the physician in charge said, 'You must realize your son has only a few months to live.' He had Hodgkin's disease. The London Clinic did all that could be done, taking him in for treatment whenever possible and sending him home for periods of recovery; but the end could not be avoided and he died in January 1959.

My wife and I came back to our own home after the funeral. We had been offered hospitality by well-meaning friends, but we thought it best instead to come back to the empty house and start learning to live with it all. About midnight there was a knock at the door, and when I answered it a messenger handed me an envelope bearing the royal cypher. Inside was a personal letter from the Queen Mother saying that she had heard of our loss, and sending her sympathy. It was typical of her immense kindness that she had made time that day to remember us in our grief. Like the king, she let nothing escape her.

In 1961 very delicate negotiations started to take place between the earl marshal and the BBC. These high-level discussions concerned the arrangements we would need to make for the coverage of the ceremonies that would surround Sir Winston Churchill's funeral. At this time the old man was still alive, but it was obvious that his funeral, when it came, would be one of the most complex and majestic that Britain had experienced, and if we were to handle it with the skill it deserved it would take months of preparation. I was asked to prepare a scheme for the ceremony to cover all the events in London, including the paying of homage, the funeral procession and the full service. It would be covered by television and sound; I planned all the microphone coverage, plotted the microphone positions and ordered the circuits to make everything perfect as a last act of justice to a great man. In the end I had retired by the time Churchill actually died, but my plans were waiting and brought straight into operation.

Postscript

In 1964 I decided that over 40 years was enough and made up my mind to retire. When I announced my decision I was asked to carry on, but I'd decided to go, and said 'I'm going to pack up' — just like that. You get to a point where you can't do or take any more. I'd become mechanized. I had done every sort of event, most of them many times over, and there did not seem to be any challenges left — or if there were, I was weary of them. I wrote to Sir Michael Adeane to inform the queen of my decision, and left the corporation in April. One of my last BBC broadcasts was on the receiving end: I was interviewed about my career and memories on 'Radio Newsreel' in March.

Shortly after I retired I was delighted to be asked to a private audience with the Queen Mother at Clarence House in Pall Mall, and with the queen later the same day at Buckingham Palace. The Queen Mother presented me with a recent, autographed photograph of herself, and the queen gave me a pair of gold monogrammed cufflinks, thanking me for my services. We have kept in touch. Barbara and I have been to their garden parties at Buckingham Palace and we are proud to get their Christmas cards every year, and on the occasions when we have met over the years it has been wonderful to keep that personal contact.

But the transition from immense high pressure to the tranquillity of retirement was a greater shock than I had expected. The first two or three years were fine: I had always been healthy and, apart from a dose of flu in 1947, I had not had any time off for sickness since I left Buxton.

But little by little Barbara noticed a slow change coming over me. I started to lose interest in things. I didn't want to do anything, although normally I can't sit still for a minute. I went very quiet, didn't want to be bothered, didn't want to see anyone, didn't want to go anywhere. I just grew depressed and listless. My wife couldn't understand it, but eventually, over a bank holiday, matters seemed to swamp me and I had a breakdown. Luckily my wife was able to get me under the wing of an excellent doctor and he put me straight into hospital. I stayed there for a month, having electric-shock therapy. Barbara came every day to see me, but I don't remember much about it. The treatment worked. So many fear electric-shock treatment; my wife had to sign papers before it was administered, taking the responsibility. But it is effective. People debunk it, but since I came out of hospital I've led a very busy, active and enjoyable life.

My doctor said the breakdown was hardly surprising. I had been kept on my nerves all the time in my

Postscript

job, for everything I did was live. You were always on your toes, expecting something to go wrong and knowing you would have to cope with it on your own with whatever makeshift solution you could devise. I had been wound up for 40 years, and paid the penalty. My doctor said it should really have happened years before, just after the war, and then it would have been someone else's responsibility.

But I recovered. At first I had to take a number of tablets every day. But one day I just felt better and said, 'That's finished. I won't take any more.' And I've been fine ever since. My doctor is delighted with me; he became a friend as well as a doctor, for I found he was a son of Archbishop Fisher, whose enthronement I had covered in the old days.

With my return to health I started to take part in local government affairs, especially educational matters. This might seem odd for someone who left school at 14, but of course I studied, and studied hard, after that; in today's schools much of what I had to learn for myself would be taught and, indeed, encouraged. I made up to some extent for my lack of formal schooling in October 1973 when I was elected a Fellow of the Royal Society of Arts.

Today I try to give special help to those young men who, like myself, have an electrical aptitude. For some years I have been a governor of Rutlish School in Merton and am now deputy chairman of the board of governors. It is old, and well endowed, so although it is now a comprehensive school with over 800 pupils, it is able to finance some excellent

A World in Your Ear

facilities. I take a particular interest in the technical aspect.

My great interest in the last decade has been in the laser. I've been watching the development of the ruby laser and the various gas lasers from the early 1960s and I believe they hold untold possibilities for the future. I am keen to see their application to the tuition stage in high school. After all, anyone nowadays can think of becoming a computer expert, and thousands are being turned out. But soon there will be a great expansion in the world of lasers, as there was in my lifetime with radio, and I would like our students to be in the vanguard of knowledge.

Of course, you cannot play about with the laser: you cannot pick up a handbook and try it out for yourself as one could with my early radio experiments. The laser is very dangerous and you have to treat it with respect. But I would like to see our pupils learning about it at least to the equivalent of the crystal radio stage, so that later they can progress to the real development work. I would like to see it on the syllabus. For the laser beam can carry all sorts of sound — many channels of music, many telephone lines — along different frequencies of light with great purity. So I joke about how much copper wire it will save, and try to push our boys into the future. Its prospects in the medical, military and precision-engineering fields are unlimited.

I have learnt, at last, to take life easy, living each day to the full, not overplanning for tomorrow, but never wasting time, for time goes on even if you do

Postscript

not, and wins the race in the end. My main hobby has always been antiques, collecting old English oak, old glass and early mechanical and electrical models, which I like to get working again; and I tend my garden. Barbara and I travel a lot: we have returned for very many years to Spain, to the same family hotel in Benidorm, and seen it grow from a small fishing village to the huge resort it is today. I like to sit with a glass on the terrace, letting the sun brown me outside and the brandy warm me inside, and I feel good.

And I like to look back on my life, from my brief schooldays and hard apprenticeship to the exhilarating days of pioneer radio. Through my work I have met an extraordinary number of people, and been warmed by unexpected and long-lasting friendships at all levels. I met many of them under conditions of stress, keyed up about a live broadcast: and it is a tribute to the good spirits of the people of Britain, great and ordinary, that my memories are so crowded and so happy.

Appendix

VIP Outside Broadcasts from London in Wartime

1939

3 Sept.	His Majesty	Buckingham Palace	1800–1805
	Prime Minister	10 Downing Street	1115–1124
7 Nov.	Lord Halifax	10 Downing Street	2115–2130
11 Nov.	Her Majesty	Buckingham Palace	2100–2105
17 Nov.	Leslie Burgin, Minister of Supply	Grosvenor House	1345–1400
23 Nov.	Dr Beneš and H.G. Wells	Grosvenor House	1335–1400
26 Nov.	Prime Minister	Central War Room	2115–2130
25 Dec.	His Majesty	Sandringham	1500–1505

1940

9 Jan.	Prime Minister	Mansion House	1445–1530
15 Feb.	Walter Elliott	Central War Room	1800–1815

Appendix

Date	Speaker	Venue	Time
23 Feb.	Speeches to men of *Ajax* and *Exeter*	Guildhall	1430–1500
13 April	Her Majesty	YWCA, Great Russell St	2145–2150
17 April	Nevile Henderson	Grosvenor House	1330–1400
23 April	Duff Cooper	Grosvenor House	1400–1425
30 April	Ronald Cross, Minister of Economic Warfare	Connaught Rooms	1400–1420
6 May	Belgian Ambassador, post-master-general and W.S. Morrison	Mayfair Hotel	2115–2145
10 May	Prime Minister	10 Downing Street	2100–2107
15/16 May	Queen Wilhelmina	Buckingham Palace	2100, 2308, 0200
19 May	Prime Minister	10 Downing Street	2100–2111
24 May	His Majesty	Buckingham Palace	2100.30–2112.30
24 May	Queen Wilhelmina	Buckingham Palace	1300–1311
26 May	Archbishop of Canterbury	St George's Hall	0830–0900

14 June	Her Majesty (in French)	Buckingham Palace	2203–2207.10
16 June	King Haakon (in Norwegian)	Buckingham Palace	1830.30–1835
17 June	Prime Minister	10 Downing Street	2100.30–2103.45
18 June	Prime Minister	10 Downing Street	2100.30–2131.45
30 June	Lord President of the Council	10 Downing Street	2045–2051
8 July	King Haakon (in English)	Buckingham Palace	2100.30–?
14 July	Prime Minister	10 Downing Street	2101–2116.55
28 July	American Ambassador, two-way conversation to Mr Franklin and others on board liner off New York	St Leonard's, Winkfield Road, Windsor	2004–2014
11 Sept.	Prime Minister	Central War Room	1800.51–1812.40
23 Sept.	His Majesty	Windsor Castle (shelter)	1800.26–1811.45
13 Oct.	TRH Princesses Elizabeth and Margaret	Windsor Castle (study)	1715–1720.30

Appendix

21 Oct.	Prime Minister, introduced by Mr du Chesne (in English and French)	Central War Room	2030–2100
21 Nov.	Mrs Churchill, introduced by Lady Croig	Central War Room	1530–1542
23 Dec.	Prime Minister	Central War Room	2100–2118
25 Dec.	His Majesty	Windsor Castle	1500.30–1509.45

1941

21 Jan.	HRH Duchess of Kent	Coppins, Iver	1744–1748
16 Feb.	Prime Minister	Chequers	2100–2138
23 Feb.	Rt Hon. R.G. Menzies, Prime Minister of Australia	Chequers	1811–1819.30
2 March	Mrs Churchill	Chequers	2040–2043.45
16 April	Prime Minister, recording for Australia	10 Downing Street	1515–1519
27 April	Prime Minister	10 Downing Street	2100.20–2133

A World in Your Ear

3 May	Prime Minister, to Poland	Chequers	2100.30–2111
12 May	Queen Marie of Yugoslavia	Great Gransden, Cambridge	0039.30–0041.50
16 June	Prime Minister, broadcast for NBC conferring honorary degree	10 Downing Street	1745.06–1749.10 (from USA), 1749.10–1759.34 (PM's reply)
17 June	Lord Beaverbrook, recordings	10 Downing Street	1200–1209.35, 1200–1211.58
22 June	Prime Minister	Chequers	2101.05–2119.18
1 July	Prime Minister, recording of handing Canadian 'Victory Loan Torch'	10 Downing Street	1705–1715
14 July	Prime Minister, luncheon speech	County Hall, London	1418.55–1448.59
1 Sept.	Kings' and presidents' broadcast: King Haakon of Norway, General	Ritz Hotel	2100–2145

Appendix

		Sikorski (PM of Poland), Professor Pieter Gerbrandy (PM of the Netherlands), M Hubert Pierlot (PM of Belgium), M Sharalambos Simopoulos (Greece) M Joseph Beck (foreign minister to Luxembourg)		
4 Sept.	Mr Mackenzie King and Prime Minister	Mansion House	1420.20– 1509.20
12 Oct.	Lord Beaverbrook	Cherkley, Leatherhead	2100.10– 2116.30
28 Oct.	Mrs Churchill	Central War Room	1816–1823.30
10 Nov.	Lord Mayor, Prime Minister and Archbishop of Canterbury	Mansion House	1400–1515

Date	Speaker	Location	Time
8 Dec.	Prime Minister	Central War Room	2101–2121
22 Dec.	Mrs Churchill	Central War Room	1815–1821
25 Dec.	His Majesty	Windsor Castle	1501–1510.9

1942

Date	Speaker	Location	Time
4 Jan.	Anthony Eden	Central War Room	2117–2132
15 Feb.	Mrs Churchill	Chequers	2040–2045
	Prime Minister	Chequers	2100.20–2126
28 March	His Majesty	Windsor Castle	2101–2110
19 April	R.C. Casey, Minister of State	Chequers	2114–2125.30
10 May	Prime Minister	10 Downing Street	2100–2137
20 Oct.	Mrs Churchill, to USA	10 Downing Street	1906–1912
21 Oct.	Lloyd George, Field-Marshal Smuts and Prime Minister	Royal Gallery, House of Lords	1630–1732
10 Nov.	Prime Minister, recording	Mansion House	1445–1505
29 Nov.	Prime Minister	Chequers	2100–2130
25 Dec.	His Majesty	Windsor Castle	1500.30–1512

Appendix

31 Dec.	Mrs Churchill	Central War Room	2116–2122

1943

1 Jan.	Mrs Churchill, for overseas	Central War Room	0930.30–0937.30
20 Feb.	Mrs Churchill	Central War Room	2109–2110.30
21 Feb.	Tribute to Red Army, with Anthony Eden	Albert Hall	1500–1722
21 March	Prime Minister	Chequers	2100.45–2147
11 April	Her Majesty	Windsor Castle	2101.06–2113.06
30 June	Prime Minister, conferring Freedom of City of London	Guildhall	1213–1309
	Prime Minister, conferring Freedom of City of London	Mansion House	1425-1441
22 July	Prime Minister and Marquis of Crewe	Liberal Club	1415–1453

A World in Your Ear

19 Oct.	Field Marshal Smuts and Lord Mayor	Guildhall	1200—1315
9 Nov.	Prime Minister, recording and live	Mansion House	1443—1515
25 Dec.	His Majesty	Windsor Castle	1502—1510.45

1944

26 March	Prime Minister	Chequers	2100.30—2147.30
11 May	Mr Mackenzie King and Prime Minister	Royal Gallery House of Lords	1500—1600
23 May	Mrs Churchill, appeal for aid to Russia	Central War Room	2117—2121.30
6 June	His Majesty, D-Day broadcast	Buckingham Palace (shelter)	2101—2106
27 June	Mrs Churchill, to USA	Central War Room	2306.30—2311.30
16 Oct.	Mrs Churchill, appeal for Russian Red Cross	Central War Room	2115—2117

Appendix

9 Nov.	Prime Minister, at Lord Mayor's Banquet, recorded and live	Mansion House	1440–1512
3 Dec.	His Majesty, stand-down of Home Guard	Windsor Castle	2100.45–2108
25 Dec.	His Majesty	Windsor Castle	1501–1508.40

1945

14 Jan.	Mrs Churchill, appeal for YWCA	Chequers	2025–2029.40
17 Feb.	Queen Wilhelmina	The Stubbings, Maidenhead	2030–2035
20 April	Prime Minister, recorded message for announcement of Allied link-up	10 Downing Street	2005–2006.30
8 May	Prime Minister, VE announcement	10 Downing Street	1500–1510
	His Majesty VE-Day speech	Buckingham Palace	2100–2110

13 May	Service of thanksgiving for victory in Europe	St Paul's Cathedral	1445–1610
	Prime Minister, speech on fifth anniversary of taking office	10 Downing Street	2100–2135
10 June	His Majesty	Hyde Park	1530–1540
15 Aug.	Prime Minister, announcement of VJ-Day	10 Downing Street	0000–0008
	His Majesty, VJ-Day speech	Buckingham Palace	2100–2108

Index

Abdication (1936), 51, 99-101, 115
Aberdeen, 46
Adeane, Lord, 121, 153, 169, 170, 173
Adler, Larry, 91
Afghanistan, 159
Aintree, 67-8
Air Training Corps, 170
Aladdin, 149
Aldershot, 159; Tattoo, 60, 62, 88, 89
Alexander, Sir Ulick, 154
Allison, George, 72
Amateur Rowing Association, 71
Ambrose, 58
American Western, 42
Andrews, Eamonn, 155
Annie Get Your Gun, 155
Armistice Day, 55, 73, 118
Attlee, Clement, 152, 153, 159
Australia, 63
Austria, 86

Babbiscombe, Captain, 126, 128
Baird Television Company, 119
Baldwin, Stanley, 57, 73, 83
Bate, Fred, 92-5, 139
Bates, Sir Percy, 83
Beatty, Earl, 73
Beaverbrook, Lord, 79-80, 137
Beethoven, Ludwig van, 40
Belgium, 56, 73-5, 168; Army, 17, 46
Bell, Mr, 29
Berlin, 159
Bernhard, Prince, 147
Bevin, Ernest, 152
Binyon, Major, 35
Bisley, 77, 159

Bismarck, 137
Black, George, 75-6, 114
Blackpool, 47, 141
Blake, George, 91
Blomfield, Mr, 74
Boat Race, 50, 69, 71, 88, 123, 164
Bombay, 62
Borritt, Commander and Sheila, 82
Bournemouth, 78; Symphony Orchestra, 39
Boyce, Sir Howard Leslie, 161
Bracken, Brendan, 137
Bretonneux, 120
Bridgewater, T. H., 119-20
Brighton: Metropole Hotel, 54
Britain, Battle of, 145-6
Britain, Festival of, 159-60
British Broadcasting Company, 27, 28, 32, 34, 35, 41, 43, 46, 47, 49, 50, 56, 62, 64; Corporation, 65-6, 67, 73, 78, 79, 80, 86, 88, 89, 91, 92, 93, 94, 96, 101, 104, 106, 109, 110, 113, 117, 118, 120, 122, 123, 124, 125, 131, 132, 135, 140, 144, 151, 157, 158, 163, 167-8, 173, 'Children's Hour', 36, 59, 168; 'Grand Goodnight', 61; Home Service, 98; Radio Newsreel, 173; Third Programme, 64
British Commonwealth Games (1958), 170
British Empire Exhibition, 53, 59, 69, 88
British European Airways, 162-3
British Legion Memorial Service, 73

A World in Your Ear

Brown, John, 21, 82, 91
Brussels, 56
Burgess, Fred, 15-16
Butcher, H., 142
Buxton, 13, 14, 17, 18, 19, 174;
  Gardens, 15-16; Grange Road,
  15; Hampson's Salerooms, 15
Buxton Advertiser, 13

Calico Printers, 34
Camberley, 159
Cambridge, 53, 69, 70, 147.
  See also Boat Race
Cameron, J. C., 35
Cammell Laird, 19, 20, 21, 23,
  27, 29, 32, 33, 48, 81
Campaign, HMS, 153
Canada, 44, 168; Army, 18
Canterbury Cathedral, 61, 107
Cape Town, 63
Carter, Mr, 128
Central Electricity Board, 170
Ceremony of the Keys, 65
Chamberlain, Neville, 125, 127,
  128, 129, 130, 132
Chapel-en-le-Frith, 14
Charles, Prince, 170
Chartwell, 161
Chelmsford, 25, 49, 52
Chequers, 125, 134, 136, 137,
  148
Chester Cathedral, 61
Chevalier, Maurice, 78
Chichester Cathedral, 61
Churchill, Lady, 137
Churchill, Sir Winston, 110, 126,
  132, 133-4, 135, 136, 137, 138,
  146, 147-8, 151, 152, 161,
  162, 169, 171-2
Cinderella, 148-9
cinemas, 78
Clydebank, 82
Cobham, Sir Alan, 63
Cohen, Edward, 94
Coleridge-Taylor, Samuel, 40
Collingwood, HMS, 89, 112
Columbia Broadcasting System,
  94
Columbo, Emilio, 58
concerts, 75
Cook, Gerald, 63, 117
Coppins, 146
Cotton, Billy, 58
Crouch, Mr, 96-8

Croydon, 144, 145
Cuba, 159
Cunard, 83
Cup Final, 72
Cushion, Celia, 91
Custard, Goss, 61

Daily Express, 79
dance bands, 50, 58, 59, 155
Daventry, 49, 50, 64
Dempsey, Jack, 54
Denham Studios, 118
Denmark, 86, 168
Depression, 80
Derby, 50, 141
Derby, Lord, 47
Derby Stakes, 72, 91, 112
Dimbleby, Richard, 122, 155-6,
  163, 166
Ditcham, Mr, 49
Dover, 74
Droitwich, 144
Dunkirk, 132
Durham Cathedral, 61
Dwelley, Dean, 61

Eastbourne, 77; Grand Hotel, 58
Eccles, Dr, 46
Eckerlsey, Captain Peter, 25-6,
  27, 28, 29, 32, 48, 49, 50, 51,
  52, 64
Eckersley, Roger, 49, 75, 91
Eckersley, Tom, 49
Eden, Sir Anthony, 161
Edward VIII, 55, 57, 86, 90, 99-101,
  108, 114-15
Eisenhower, Dwight D., 161
Electrical Trades Union, 23
Elizabeth, Queen Consort of
  George VI, 101, 102, 106, 108,
  111, 115, 151, 155-6, 158, 160,
  165, 167, 169, 171, 173
Elizabeth II, 53, 106, 148-50,
  151, 155-6, 157, 167, 168, 170,
  173
Elstree Studios, 118
Ely Cathedral, 61
Eurovision Song Contest, 75

Ferodo, 14
Ferranti, 43
Firebrace, Commander, 82, 97
Firth, 21
Fisher, Archbishop, 175

190

Index

5XX, 50, 64
Fleet's Lit Up, The, 114
Fleming, Dr A. P. M., 25
Flying Scotsman, 24, 149
Fogg, Eric, 39
Ford, Sir Edward, 121
France, 92, 101, 105, 121, 132, 147, 163, 168
Franks, Mr, 42
Fraser, Sir Ian, 137
Froude, Mr, 14

Gamages, 152
Gaulle, General Charles de, 147-8
General Electric Company, 30, 43
General Post Office, 24, 36, 40, 45, 48, 59, 66, 88, 97-8, 99, 104, 118, 119, 125, 126
General Strike (1926), 56-7, 128
George V, 53, 57, 83, 86, 89, 90, 112, 114, 167; Silver Jubilee (1935), 87
George VI, 101-24, 130, 144, 147, 150, 151, 153, 154, 155-6, 158, 160, 165, 166-7, 169
Geraldo, 58
Germany, 76, 86, 92, 129, 131, 140, 144, 146, 168
Gerrard, Gene, 63
Gibbons, Carroll, 58
Gibbons, W. M., 20
Gilberthorpe, Mr, 29
Glasgow, 80, 90, 91
Glendenning, Raymond, 155
Godfrey, Dan, 36, 39, 40, 44, 45
Godfrey, Sir Dan, 39
Good, Meyrick, 68-9
Grand National, 67-9, 112
Great Exhibition (1851), 159
Grimesthorpe, 21
Groot, de, 58
Guildford Cathedral, 62
Guinness, 159

Haley, Sir William, 157
Hall, C. M., 91
Hall, Henry, 91
Hallé Orchestra, 39, 43
Handley, Tommy, 150
Hanson, O. B., 94
Harper, Commander, 89
Hardinge, Sir Alexander, 109, 121
Harrison, Beatrice, 67
Harrison, Major, 141

Harrods, 70
Henley Royal Regatta, 71, 159
Herbert, A. P., 82
Hess, Rudolf, 137
Heston Airport, 125
Heysham, 32
Hilversum, 61
Hirsch, Lionel, 39
His Master's Voice, 65
Hitler, Adolf, 124, 125, 127, 128, 129, 136, 137, 159
Holland, 86, 92, 168
Home, Sir Alec Douglas, 125, 161
Hopkins, Harry, 137
How It Works, 14
Howard, J. P., 91
Hudson, Mr, 139

Imperial Airways, 123
Imperial War Graves Commission, 73-4
Independent Television Authority, 168
India Bill (1935), 132
Indian Broadcasting Company, 62
Institute of Electrical Engineers, 28, 29, 63-4
Institute of Radio Engineers, 63-4
International Trunk Exchange, 104
Ipswich: St Matthew's Baths, 143
Iran, 159
Iraq, 159
Ireland, 74, 155
Irwin, Lord, 62
Ismay, General Lord, 126
Italy, 86
ITMA, 150

Jellicoe, Lord, 73
Juliana, Queen, 147

Kennedy, Joseph, 138, 139
Kent, Duchess of, 87
Kent, Duke of, 83, 86, 106, 155, 157
King-Hall, Stephen, 87
Knight, Mr, 29
Korea, 159

Larcombe, Major D. R., 72
Lascelles, Sir Alan, 121
lasers, 176
Le Clanché batteries, 15
Leigh, Sir Piers, 121

191

A World in Your Ear

Leopold, King, 74
Lewis's, 34
licences, 66
Lichtenstein, 159
Liddell, Alvar, 130
Lincoln Cathedral, 61
Lincolnshire Handicap, 72
Lindsay, A. D., 52-3
Litt, Mr, 49
Liverpool, 47; Cathedral, 61; Lord Street, 44; University, 46
London: Alexandra Palace, 117, 118, 119; Battersea Power Station, 81; Big Ben, 107-8, 133-4, 160; Blitz, 145-6; Broadcasting House, 69, 88, 97, 104, 105, 110, 111, 112, 116, 124, 125, 127, 128, 129, 130, 131, 146, 153, 160, 166; Buckingham Palace, 101, 104, 105, 109, 121, 125, 126, 127, 130, 139, 146, 147, 151, 153, 154, 157, 158, 160, 165, 168, 169, 170, 173; Cavour restaurant, 58; Cenotaph, 47, 73, 105, 110, 118; Central War Room, 126, 127, 128, 131, 136, 138, 147; Chapel Mews, 123; Clarence House, 173; Claridges, 157; Clifton Hotel, 127, 131; Crystal Palace, 96-8; Daly's Theatre, 63; Downing Street, 57, 125, 126, 129, 130, 133, 138, 152, 154; Great Portland Street, 111, 124; Guildhall, 156; Holborn Empire, 75; Houses of Parliament, 63, 107, 133; Leicester Square, 58, 63, 71; Lords, 72; Mayfair Ballroom, 58; Metropole Hotel, 58; Middlesex Guildhall, 104; Old Vic, 64; Oval, 72; Pagani's restaurant, 111; Palladium, 75, 76; Piccadilly Hotel, 58; Portland Place, 153, 166; St James's Palace, 55, 90, 101, 108, 126; St Paul's Cathedral, 73, 87, 90; Savoy Hill, 28, 48, 50, 56, 57, 59, 64, 71; Storey's Gate, 126, 136, 137; Tower of London, 64-5; Trafalgar Square, 108, 145; Westminster Abbey, 83-6, 104, 105, 108, 157, 161, 168; Westminster Hall, 89; YWCA, 82; Zoo, 59, 69, 118

London Clinic, 171
London Fire Brigade, 82
London Polytechnic, 159
Lord Mayor's Banquet, 50, 160-1
Love Parade, The, 78
Luton, 141
Lyons, 159

MacDonald, Ramsay, 88
Machin, Mr, 29
Macmillan, Harold, 161
Madam Butterfly, 39
Magician, 70
Manchester, 25, 28, 32, 33, 36, 38, 40, 44, 45. 46, 47, 73, 92, 113, 118; Athenaeum Club, 46; City Hall, 46; College of Technology, 46; Dickenson Street, 34, 38, 40; Free Trade Hall, 43; Midland Hotel, 43; Oxford Street, 37, 38, 42; Oxford Street Cinema, 42-3; Palatine restaurant, 37-8;Piccadilly Cinema, 43; St Peter's Square, 47; Trafford Park, 25, 34; War Memorial, 47
Manchester Evening Chronicle, 46
Mantovani, 58
Marconi Company, 25, 27, 35, 43, 49, 50, 52, 54
Marconi-EMI Television Company, 117, 119, 120
Marconi-Reisz, 55
Marconi-Sykes, 54
Margaret, Princess, 148-50, 151, 155-6
Margate, 77
Marina, Princess, 83, 86, 146, 157
Marshall, Howard, 81, 85-7, 105, 155
Marshall, Percival, 15
Mary, Queen, 82-3, 86, 100
Maufe, Sir Edward, 62
Maurois, André, 105
Menin Gate, 73-4, 75
Mersey, River, 68
Merton, 75-6, 80, 96, 115, 134, 145, 167, 175
Metropolitan Vickers, 25, 34
microphones, 40, 41, 42, 53, 54, 55, 58, 59, 65, 67, 94, 102, 110, 132, 157
Miéville, Sir Eric, 121
Mitcham, 145; High School, 144

Index

Morecambe Musical Festival, 45
Morrison, Herbert, 145, 152
Morrison, T. H., 39
Morshead, Sir Owen, 53
Munich, 125, 128
Murrow, Ed, 139, 145-6
Mussolini, Benito, 136

National Broadcasting Company 92, 94
Nelson, HMS, 112, 114
Nelson, Lord, 30
Nelson, Mr, 29-30
New York, 63, 90, 93, 95; 5th Avenue, 93; Fire Brigade, 95, 96; St Regis Hotel, 93
Nicholls, Basil E., 114
Nickalls, Gully, 71

OB7, 123, 124
Oklahoma!, 155
Old Mother Red Riding Boots, 149
Olympic Games: 13th, 159; 14th, 158-9
Ostend: Kursaal, 75
outside broadcasts, early, 41, 42, 43 43, 44, 46-7, 50, 57, 66-73, 77, 81-2
Oxford, 141; University, 52-3, 69, 70, 71. *See also* Boat Race

Palmer, Dr, 46
Paris, 93, 121, 122
Partridge, Mr, 54
Pearl Harbor, 146
Peck, Geoffrey, 164
Peterborough Park Laundry, 142
Philip, Prince, 157, 169
Pinewood Studios, 118
Plumer, Field-Marshal Lord, 73
Pointer, Jack, 23
Poland, 127
Portsmouth, 88, 112
Practical Mechanics and Electricity, 14
Preston, Sir Harry, 54
Preston, W. G., 91
propaganda, 146

Queen Mary, 82, 83, 90, 91, 92

Radio City, 94

Radio Communication Company, 35, 92
Radio Corporation of America, 78, 80
Radio Times, 71
Rance, George, 128
Ratcliffe, Reginald, 24
Rayes Park County School, 144
Reading: People's Pantry, 142
Reith, Sir John, 29, 52, 55-6, 57, 62, 67, 79, 80, 83, 86, 98, 99, 100, 101, 102, 110, 114, 120, 121, 122, 132, 133, 157, 158
Robinson, Commander, 89
Round, Captain, 49
Rowan, Leslie, 153
Roy, Harry, 58
Royal, Frank, 92
Royal Air Force, 131, 136, 138
Royal Command Performances, 76, 150
Royal Navy, 89, 90, 112
Royal Society of Arts, 175
Royal Sovereign, 88
Rutlish School, 175

Saerchinger, C., 94
Sandler, Albert, 58
Sandringham, 86, 89, 114, 115, 158, 169
Sandwich, 94
Savoy Hotel Orpheans, 59
Scarborough: Poor Law Institution, 141
Schuster, Leonard, 117
Scotland, 46, 80, 137
Scott, Sir Giles, 62
Selfridge's, 55, 56, 64
Seth-Smith, David, 59
Sheffield, 18-19, 20, 21, 24, 28, 29, 31, 36, 44, 142; Everton Road, 20; Hunters Bar, 20; University, 20, 21, 25
Sheffield Daily Telegraph, 18
Sheper, Klinton, 45
Shrewsbury Castle, 142
Simpson, Wallis, 90, 99
Smithe, Victor, 36
Smuts, General, 137
Snagge, John, 91, 105
'sound pictures', 81, 90
South Africa, 155-6
Southampton, 91, 92

193

A World in Your Ear

Southport, 44; Cambridge Hall, 45; Infirmary, 45; Lord Street, 47
Southsea Castle, 88, 112
Spithead, 88
sport, 50, 66-72, 94-5, 118, 155. *See also under individual events*
Squire, Sir John, 71
stereophony, 64
Stobart, J. C., 61
Swann, Mr, 49
Swindon, 142

Tanar, Hubert, 148-9
television, 117-19, 120, 127
Thames, River, 60, 63, 70, 81, 82, 89, 101
Topham, Mirabelle, 67-8
theatres, 63, 66, 75
Tresmand, Ivy, 63
Tunbridge Wells, 77
Twickenham, 66, 67
2LO 45, 64
2ZY, 36, 44, 46, 92; Orchestra, 44

Union Grinding Works, 44
United States of America, 38, 46, 68, 78, 86, 92, 93, 94, 104, 139, 140, 145-6, 168

Vanguard, HMS, 155
variety, 75, 114
VE Day, 151
Victoria, Queen, 147, 159

Wakelam, Captain Teddy, 66
Water Lily, The, 82
Watt, John, 91

Wellington, Sir Lindsay, 122-3
Wembley, 53, 59, 69, 72, 88
West, Captain, 64
Westerham, 134, 162
White, Jimmy, 63
Wilhelmina, Queen of the Netherlands, 146-7
Wilhelmina, Queen of Romania, 147
Wimbledon, 72, 118, 119
Winchester Cathedral, 61
Windsor: Castle, 89-90, 99-100, 117, 125, 149, 150, 158, 167; Great Park, 159; Royal School, 148; Winkfield Road, 138
Wood, Barbara, *wife*, 30-3, 47, 55, 56, 62, 67, 74, 122, 144, 145, 162, 171, 173, 174, 177
Wood, Dorothy, *sister*, 16, 26, 122
Wood, Patricia, *daughter*, 74, 122, 144
Wood, Mr and Mrs Robert, *parents*, 13, 14, 16, 17, 18, 19, 20, 21, 26, 28, 29, 30-3, 34, 52, 80, 122
Wood, William Henry, *son*, 74, 122, 144-5, 170-1
Woodroffe, Lieutenant-Commander Tommy, 112-14
Wookey Hole, 94
Worsley, Francis, 150
Wright, Kenneth, 25
Writtle, 25-6, 28

York: Minster, 61; Museum, 142
Ypres, 73, 74
Yugoslavia, 86
Yvonne, 63

Zeppelins, 19